Invincible You

Discover Your Inner Power and Achieve Your Heart's Desires

By Dr. Alexander Avila

Heart and Soul Publishing International

2018

ISBN-10: 0692043381

ISBN-13: 978-0692043387

ACKNOWLEDGEMENTS

Special Thanks and Love To:

Antonio, My Father, the Great Philosopher: May your spirit rest in creativity and peaceful joy.

Jenny, My Muse of Artistry: May your loving energy and enthusiasm for life spread across the world.

Andrew, My Son, the Great Innovator: May your ideas help humanity and create greatness in the universe.

Itzy, My Four-Legged Ball of Love and Nurturing: You light up my day.

Praise for *Invincible You*

"Join Dr. Avila on a journey to Invincible Mountain—the inner mental place where you can achieve your greatest dreams and fulfill your most wondrous potential. In his groundbreaking book, *Invincible You*, Dr. Avila does the improbable: Giving you the psychological and spiritual tools to transform your life while encouraging you to be the very best that you already are. A masterwork of self-transformation."

Dr. Hendrie Weisinger, performance psychologist and two-time New York Times bestselling author, *Performing Under Pressure: The Science of Doing Your Best When It Matters*
www.hankweisingerphd.com

"Dr. Avila's new book, *Invincible You*, offers timeless loving wisdom to help you live a good, balanced, and happy life. He simplifies principles and gives brief exercises to help you integrate them into your daily life. By exercising patience muscles, getting your time back, overcoming your rush and fear weaknesses, and much more, you'll reconnect with your true Invincible self and learn to love your life again."

Dr. Paulette Sherman, author of *The Book of Sacred Baths: 52 Bathing Rituals to Revitalize Your Spirit*
www.drpaulettesherman.com

"Who doesn't want to be Invincible? In his book *Invincible You*, Dr. Avila takes us by the hand and identifies a range of weaknesses that act as bullies, controlling our emotions and behaviors. Each chapter teaches us how to overcome those weaknesses and become the masters of our destiny, free to live the life we desire. Take time to absorb each lesson along the way, and give yourself wholeheartedly to the process. You will relish your own self-discovery as you emerge, Invincible You!"

Dr. Mary Jayne Rogers, author of *From Overwhelmed to Inspired: Your Personal Guide to Health and Well-Being*
www.doctormaryjayne.com

"*Invincible You* is the key to achieving your greatest desires in life. Dr. Avila really breaks it down so *anyone* can achieve success. He gives you a full plate to digest with quick bites, the main course, and dessert *literally* in this book. If you want to discover the star player that lives within us all, and learn to live like a champion, *Invincible You* is a must read. Dr. Alex delivers the goods to help you begin your Invincible life."

Mario Rivers, author, speaker, relationship advisor, business
coach, and founder of Online Business
Startup University
www.mariorivers.com

"Dr. Avila's *Invincible You* teaches us the right way to connect with others and teaches readers how to move from the Mind of Scarcity to the Mind Of Abundance; one of the 7 mindsets of a Connector."

Michelle Tillis Lederman: Forbes Top 25 Networking
Expert and best-selling author of *The 11 Laws of Likability*
and *The Connector's Advantage: 7 Mindsets to Grow Your
Influence and Impact*
www. MichelleTillisLederman.com

TABLE OF CONTENTSiii

PART ONE

DAY TRIPS TO INVINCIBLE MOUNTAIN

Chapter One

Your Invincible Mind

Here's an important fact that applies to you: You have an Invincible Mind and a Self-Defeating Mind.

The Invincible Mind is the part of your mind that is incapable of being defeated; its inherent nature is to win, to thrive, and to love. It dwells on your success, growth, and contribution. It is kind and compassionate to you—forgiving you for your mistakes, loving you despite the circumstances.

The Self-Defeating Mind is the part of your mind that is easily defeated because it dwells on the negative, the bad, and the failures in your life. It focuses on your disappointments, regrets, fears, and sadness. It is unkind to you and judges you harshly, mercilessly, relentlessly.

The Invincible Mind thinks of reasons why you can do something. The Self-Defeating Mind thinks of reasons why you can't. When your Self-Defeating Mind is in charge, you miss opportunities, or if you see them, you don't have the willpower or courage to take action. When your Invincible Mind is in control, you catch opportunities even before they arise, and then act decisively upon them.

When your Self-Defeating Mind rules, you only have wishes; when your Invincible Mind predominates, you have willpower and a firm, secure vision of what you desire.

Which mind is most prevalent in you?

In reality, you probably have a combination of both. Part of your mind wants you to succeed and focuses on your positive attributes. The other part tells you why you can't do something, or can't be somebody, and leads you to failure and futility.

Your Invincible Mind says, "You've got this. You are smart, beautiful, loving, and talented. You will achieve your dreams."

Your Self-Defeating Mind says, "You can't do this. You're not smart enough, attractive enough, loving enough, or talented enough. You're going to fail."

In the constant battle for mental supremacy, your two opposing thought forces fight each other in vicious, yet subtle, ways.

Sometimes, your Invincible Mind wins, and you experience a surge of power, timelessness, and compassion. You act with passion and go for what you truly want: a relationship, career, or lifestyle advancement.

Other times, your Self-Defeating Mind is on top, and you plummet into sadness, frustration, and a sense of futility—leaving behind your most treasured dreams and goals—and settling for something much less desirable.

How do you permanently establish your Invincible Mind so your days are cheery and your accomplishments are real and lasting?

You need to take a trip to Invincible Mountain.

From Neurotic Village to Invincible Mountain

There once was an unhappy man named Walter who lived in Neurotic Village. Neurotic Village was a place full of bitter, complaining, envious, fearful, and angry people.

Born in Neurotic Village, and raised by worried and critical parents, the unhappy boy, Walter, grew up to become the unhappy man, Walter. His life was full of pain, regret, and despair. No matter how much he accomplished in the material world—money, career success, or social approval—he still felt like a failure.

One day, there was a visitor from Invincible Mountain—a beautiful place where the people were content, loving, and peaceful. Hearing strange and wondrous stories of this place where everyone got along, and men and women lived in harmony and happiness, Walter had a strong desire to visit and learn more.

He packed a suitcase and began the journey to Invincible Mountain.

When he arrived, he was hospitably greeted and taken to the mayor of Invincible Mountain, a petite middle-aged woman dressed in simple, yet attractive, clothes. With inviting eyes and a warm smile, she told her story:

"Once, a long time ago, I, too, lived in Neurotic Village. My life was about competition, anger, and fear. I wanted more of everything I could obtain, and I didn't care who or what got in my way.

Then, I met a wise teacher, and I began to study the secrets of happiness that led me to Invincible Mountain.

I learned the simple secrets that unlocked the doors of my joy and success:

I Found Happiness by Helping Others Find It

I realized that my selfishness was a crutch that I relied on to build my false self-esteem. At the same time, the selfishness crutch kept me feeling weak and powerless. I was so busy worrying about myself—about getting what I wanted from others—that I had little energy to accomplish the true desires of my heart.

Finally, when I threw away the crutch of my selfishness, and began feeling compassion for other people—helping the needy and contributing to my community—I suddenly felt free; I saw my potential and power grow.

The more I helped others, the happier I felt.

Every time I gave my time, energy, and resources to help someone who truly needed it, I felt my own resources grow. I was no longer envious, worried, or regretful. I saw others as being like me, and I like them.

There was no need to rush, fight, or worry over things—there was more than enough for everyone.

I finally realized that the Creator had given us all an abundance of everything we needed; all we had to do was help each other find it."

Pausing with a smile of encouragement, the Mayor of Invincible Mountain continued:

I Forgave Myself for All the Past and All My Future

"Before, I was very critical of myself. I would regret past mistakes or failures—broken relationships, unwise business ventures, poor lifestyle choices—and I would become bitter and disillusioned. I would fear making more mistakes in the future, which kept me limited and afraid of taking risks. I felt trapped and weak.

But, then I realized something. I understood that when I made a so-called mistake in the past, I was at a certain grade level in my psychological development, say, fifth grade. The mistakes I made were fifth grade mistakes—when I was cruel to a loved one; when I stayed in the wrong relationship too long; when I refused to believe in the dreams of my excellence.

It took some time, but as I raised my psychological and spiritual grade level, I knew I wouldn't make the same mistakes. I understood that I would act from a higher level of knowledge and wisdom. In college, I would no longer be making elementary school errors—choosing the wrong relationships, and so forth. I would select the right people and circumstances to enter my life. I would manage my emotions better and learn how to successfully deal with obstacles and setbacks.

With this new understanding, I began to forgive myself for any real or imagined errors I had made in the past, or would make in the future. Every day, I decided to forgive myself and learn from my experiences, so I could be more loving and optimistic about myself.

Soon, I found that I was not only making fewer mistakes, but that others were more optimistic and loving toward me because I was that way toward myself first. By learning to love myself and practice self-forgiveness, I was finally free to express my love for others.

Forgiveness became my daily companion."

Now the Invincible Mountain mayor's entire face beamed in a most magnificent way as she summarized the third and final lesson of Invincibility:

Gratitude Became My Best Friend

"Instead of asking for more, I gave thanks for the riches I already possessed. I gave thanks for my life, my happy experiences, my loved ones, and my God-given abilities in life.

I no longer prayed solely for material things or wealth. As a result, I now have more material wealth than I could ever need. And, my greatest riches come from those people I have helped to live truly and grow wondrously.

Each day, I gave thanks for the amazing feelings of gratitude I was experiencing. Each day, I realized that my life was complete. There was no lack, failure, or frustration. There was only abundance, success, and love."

As the mayor of Invincible Mountain finished her talk, she welcomed Walter to live permanently in their simple beautiful paradise. With a tender embrace and a loving voice, she concluded:

"By the way, this place we live in is not a physical land or defined territory. Invincible Mountain exists in our minds. It cannot be stolen or lost; it cannot be broken into or taken. It is always here, inside us, forever, in our minds and hearts."

Three Steps to Invincibility

Now it's your turn: Are you ready to make your permanent dwelling in Invincible Mountain by following the three secrets to your inner well-being? All you have to do is give two weeks' notice to Neurotic Village and pack your bags.

To begin your new life of Invincibility, you need to take three important steps:

1. **Give What You Want Most**
2. **Forgive Yourself**
3. **Practice Gratitude Daily**

Let's begin with a new way of thinking when it comes to obtaining what you want: Give what you want most.

1. Give What You Want Most

This is one of the greatest secrets of a successful and happy life. If you want money, you need to give more money to others. If you want love, you need to give more love to others.

This does two things.

First, it liberates your tight and constrained energy so that your energy flows outwardly instead of inwardly. Instead of being obsessed with your own flaws and inadequacies, you see the amazing possibilities that life has to offer you. By expanding your energy in this way, you focus more on the positive aspects of life, instead of the negative. Your mindset moves from anxiety and sadness to hope and optimism.

Second, giving what you want most attracts people and favorable circumstances to you because you are increasing your positive output into the world. The good you do will be returned to you—often in surprising ways.

The person you help in a loving way may not return the favor, but it may be someone else, even a bystander, who will return the love and appreciation back to you. People you don't even know may give you benefits and gifts without you having to ask for anything. The world will work in your favor to bring you the results you want.

Try it this week and see what happens:

If you want more love, be more loving: Smile at other people, be a better listener, offer sincere compliments. Visualize your love extending outward to others and feel the warmth of your loving energy as you share it with other people.

If you want more money, start looking for ways you can contribute your time and money to worthy causes and charities.

Although you may be afraid to give money when you don't have much, this is exactly the way to reverse your fear mindset into one of faith and prosperity. The results will astound you as you attract more money and goodwill into your life.

Betsy, a single schoolteacher in her early-30s, was tight with her money. She had grown up with a mother who always told her that "Money doesn't grow on trees," and "If you're not careful, you're going to end up broke like your daddy." Her father had been a fun-loving man who liked to drink and had squandered all of their savings before he left them. Although Betsy could understand her mother's point, she didn't want to end up bitter and fearful like her—always watching every penny and afraid to enjoy life.

After learning about the principle of "Give what you want most" in a workshop, Betsy decided to try it. She wanted more money and love in her life so she started applying the principle of giving away what she wanted.

Although it was hard at first, she started being more generous and open-hearted to others. She gave more money at Sunday church services, and would give some money to the homeless people she encountered—before she would walk away, thinking, "They should get a job."

As she gave more, Betsy began feeling better about herself and decided to do even more. She began volunteering at church and donated some of her clothes and personal items to charity.

Eventually, she met a nice man at church whom she ended up marrying, and they started a volunteer ministry to help the homeless. Now her favorite phrase is, "Money may not grow on trees, but love grows everywhere."

2. Forgive Yourself

Although forgiving others can be difficult, one of the hardest things to do is to forgive ourselves. We tend to be hardest on ourselves when it comes to our mistakes and weaknesses. When we are self-critical and self-condemning, our self-belief suffers (the way we feel about ourselves). We don't think we're good enough to succeed in life. We place a magnifying glass on all of our errors and create tension within our mind and body. This tension then pressures us to act in a foolish or unprepared way that leads us to poor decisions and self-defeating actions—thereby causing us to do something we really regret. As a consequence, we fall back into a bad habit or unproductive emotional pattern.

A vicious cycle has been created. The less we forgive ourselves, the more we do things that we regret because our low self-belief matches the self-harming actions that we undertook. A depressed person will only act in ways that lead to more depression; a mistake-prone person will keep repeating the same mistakes. We do what we already have inside our minds.

The way to break this downward spiral is to forgive ourselves for past mistakes and setbacks. When we do this, we can set a course for a positive and regret-free future.

> *Andrew, a college student, never felt good enough. His father was a high-achieving lawyer who was always pushing Andrew to go to college, even though Andrew struggled in school and barely managed C's. As a result, Andrew always felt guilty and regretful when he didn't do well on his exams. He was close to dropping out, and even felt suicidal at times, because Andrew felt he couldn't live up to his father's grand expectations for him (Andrew's father wanted him to become a Wall Street lawyer).*
>
> *One day a friend who had turned her life around—she had been a former drug addict—told Andrew about a new way to*

live: "Forgive yourself even before you do something that you think is a mistake."

Initially, Andrew was wary of this strange advice, yet it seemed somehow intriguing. Andrew thought: "What if I forgive myself for my bad grades, for my dislike of school, for letting my father down, for my failures in life?"

Suddenly, Andrew felt a tremendous weight released from his mind. He further thought: "If I can forgive myself for any real or imagined mistakes, then I can be free to live my life any way I want. I don't have to feel bad about what I do if I am doing what is right for me."

With this powerful new insight, Andrew decided to leave college and focus full-time on his passion of being a video game designer. He loved technology and video games, and he realized that he would be much happier—and less regretful—following his passion. Although his dad still wants him to go back to college, Andrew is blissfully doing what he loves to do, and he has never been happier.

Begin today by forgiving yourself for any real or imagined mistakes you have made in the past, or will make in the future.

Like the mayor of Invincible Mountain, recognize that you were at a lower mental grade level (e.g. the fifth grade) when you were cruel to that person; when you were defensive and touchy and lost a good job opportunity; when you were overly critical with your children, mate, or friends.

As you raise your psychological level to the 7th, 8th, 9th grades and beyond, you will learn how to avoid making the same errors. You will have more command over your thoughts and feelings. You will become a graduate student of Invincibility.

3. Practice Gratitude Daily

Psychology researchers have shown that practicing daily gratitude can provide significant mental health benefits. According to a study published in *Applied Psychology: Health and Well-Being*, grateful people sleep better (Digdon & Koble, 2011). In a study conducted at the University of Kentucky, it was found that grateful people have more empathy and less aggression (Dewall, Lambert, Pond, Kashdan, & Fincham, 2011).

When you are grateful, you are deeply appreciative of the kindness or benefits you have received. You are infused with feelings of contentment, love, and appreciation that go far beyond mere words. It's true: Gratitude can become a feeling of immense joy and ecstasy.

On the other hand, when we are not grateful or appreciative of what we have in this life, we tend to become bitter, demanding, frustrated, and envious. We ask ourselves, "Why do other people get all the good luck and benefits while we're stuck with the rotten leftovers?"

In reality, that is the wrong question to ask. Instead ask, "How can I give thanks for all I have already been given?" This question liberates you from a self-centered mindset and puts your attention on the goodness of the Universe. Although there is evil and failure in the world, gratitude represents the good, the pure, and the beautiful.

Gratitude is a trait that Invincible people possess in abundance. Invincible people give thanks for everything they receive because it reverses their focus from "Poor Me" to "Blessed Me." They can even be grateful for negative occurrences because they can learn something from them and become stronger as a result.

Start today by keeping a Gratitude Journal. Every day, write down three things you are grateful for: Your life, family, friends, children, pets, health, home, or job. Be grateful for your looks or intelligence, your creativity or talents, your contributions to the world, and your positive experiences in life.

Even if you are lacking in some of these things, and believe there is little to be grateful about, you can still feel blessed for the simplest of things: the air you breathe, the sun that warms you, the birds that sing, the nature that soothes, the beauty of newborn babies or animals, the love between lovers, the creativity of an artist, the spirituality of those who seek Truth, and the beauty of a life that gives you a slice of eternity to place your mark on the world and leave a lasting legacy of love.

Keep your Gratitude Journal for a couple of weeks and notice the positive changes in your life. You will have more energy, optimism, and courage than ever before. You will see life from an entirely different perspective, the Invincible Mind way, in which you are constantly expanding and bringing more light and excellence into the world.

Soon, you will be expressing gratitude every moment you are alive because of the wonderful way it makes you feel, and the new benefits that effortlessly come into your life.

Journey to Your Invincible Mind

Remember, the three steps to enhance your Invincible Mind:

1. **Give What you Want Most**
2. **Forgive Yourself**
3. **Practice Gratitude Daily**

With these steps as your guide, you will soon be on your way to your deepest fulfillments and your greatest joy.

Chapter Two

The 7% Club of the Living

Look at yourself in the mirror and rejoice: You are alive. You are one of the miracles of the Earth.

Think about this: It is estimated that approximately 107 billion people have lived on earth (Haub, 1995). With a current population estimated at around 7 billion, that means there are roughly 15 dead people for every person who is alive. If you are alive now, which I presume you are if you're reading this book, you're one of those lucky 7%—those who are currently living.

What an amazing statistic this is. You are a member of the 7% Club of the Living rather than being in the 93% Club of the Dead. This means that this is your window of life opportunity—your time to do everything you have always wanted to do in life. There is no time for excuses, laments, or fears.

Your time to live is now.

Think of the term "life." We throw it around all the time without really understanding its significance. We say phrases such as, "Live your life." "Your life." "My life." Yet, words can't even begin to describe the beauty, amazement, and majesty of being alive in the present time, the present moment.

Take a deep breath and ponder the reality: By being alive at this very moment, you are breathing, walking, working, making love, giving love, receiving love, creating, and sharing experiences and beautiful moments. All of these marvelous things are possible only because you are presently alive.

Rejoice: You are one of the 7%. One of the Living.

Incredible! Let it sink in right now. You are alive.

Take another deep breath and meditate on the billions who have died, and are no longer living. They may have lived amazing, productive, loving, and happy lives. Or, they may have lived suffering and defeated lives that were a living hell. Regardless of what they enjoyed or suffered, they were once alive, and now they are dead.

Visualize some of their lives—their accomplishments and failures; their loves and hates; their loved ones; their children, dreams, and devastations. You may begin to feel great compassion for these long-dead souls, while at the same time feeling joy and gratitude that you are still in the realm of the living.

All of the recognized and esteemed people on Earth in history are now in the Club of the Dead. Their light shone brightly while they were here on Earth, and now they are gone. Soon—far sooner than you may think—you will be dead. That is not a depressing thought, but a liberating one. Regardless of your beliefs in an afterlife, your time on Earth in your body is limited.

Now what? Now, it's time to take your life into your hands and do what you've always dreamed of doing. Think about it: What do you really want to do in your life right now?

Do you want to go to the Himalayas and meditate? Do you want to fly an airplane? Invent something to change the world? Teach the young? Travel the world? Help the needy? Be an amazing parent, friend, or lover? Live healthy, free, and joyful? This is your time to do what you've always dreamed of.

What about the problems and obstacles in life? Health issues, relationship breakups, financial and career failures. Although you will face challenges and setbacks, and may suffer pain and disappointment along the way, the idea is to expand your mental panorama. Instead of being mired in the difficulties and problems of life, you will see the big picture. When you focus on the good things you can experience and accomplish as a member of the 7% Club of the Living, you will uplift your mindset. You will realize how you can make a positive difference in the world as long as you have this miracle called "Life."

Always remember that this is your window of opportunity to do anything you have ever wanted to do. By fulfilling your dreams and living with goodness and love, you will leave a lasting legacy for your children and their children to come. Soon, it will be their time to take over the sunlight of the living and carry on the positive example you have given them.

It's your turn now to live with maximum joy and excellence: to create lasting memories that will last far beyond your life on Earth.

Think of life as a brief time when the sun shines overhead. Everything is clear, beautiful, and bright. Then, the sun moves to a new spot and illuminates other people. It is their lifetime, and so on. What you accomplish during the light of day is your life legacy and can be a thing of beauty and amazement.

Practice repeating this phrase to yourself every day: "I am alive. I am the 7%. This is my time."

When you repeat this phrase daily, you will jolt yourself out of your self-hypnosis of "stuckness": that pity party of regrets, fears, sadness, and disappointments.

You will yank yourself away from bad habits, negative thoughts and behaviors, and even addictions. You will see yourself as a living and breathing entity who has the miracle of life—one of the 7%. You have the power to make your life anything you want it to be.

Maya was a middle-aged housewife whose youngest child had recently gone away to college. Although she had a loving relationship with her husband, she felt bored and lonely now that her children had grown up and moved away. She sensed that something was missing in her life, but she didn't know exactly what it was.

After learning about the "7% Club of the Living" concept, she had a sudden realization: "I may have another 30 or 40 good years left of life, and then I'll be gone. I need to do something with this precious life I have."

With her new mindset of living fully and consciously, Maya decided to go back to college and take some courses in a subject she was passionate about: Asian Art History—she had been an art and history double major in college. Excelling in her new academic environment, she made new friends and discovered a renewed enthusiasm for learning.

Eventually, she began traveling to Asian countries with her husband, and she started to savor life again—joyously enjoying every moment of her time as a member of the 7% Club.

When you are a member of the 7% Club of the Living, you will be living a paradox.

On one hand, you will take yourself and your life seriously. On the other hand, you won't take yourself so seriously. You will take your life seriously in that you recognize that your time on Earth is limited, and you need to put your talents and abilities to good use to help yourself and others.

Although you live with purpose and integrity, you also don't take yourself or your life too seriously as a member of the 7% Club. You don't worry so much about every little traffic jam, every perceived rejection, every minor setback. You think in a bigger perspective; you ask yourself: How important will this be 50 years from today, 5 years from today, even 5 weeks from today. Chances are, not very important—you probably won't even remember it. Now you start to realize that small things don't need to overwhelm your life and rob your precious peace of mind; you are something far greater than your problems.

You are alive.

Remind yourself each day: "I am a member of the esteemed 7% Club of the Living. My motto is to live each day consciously, joyfully, and with love, as I help others do the same."

And, yes, there is that word again, Love. Love is the one thing, the one essence, that you want to fill your life with. Love is that amazing feeling of elevation, compassion, and connection with all of the humans who are now living, and who have ever lived. That is the part of your 7% life that will last forever in the hearts and minds of those you touch while you are on this planet.

Now we are coming to the end of this chapter, but not to the end of your life. Not yet, anyway. You are still here, breathing, learning, loving, and growing. It's your time to celebrate. No matter how many times the words are said, they are always sweet to hear: You are part of the 7% Club of the Living. When you wake up each morning; when you go to sleep at night; say these words to yourself with passion, confidence, and love:

"I am one of the 7%.

My time to live is now.

The sun shines on me today. Tomorrow it may go elsewhere, but as long as I am here on this Earth, I will enjoy every drop of life that I have—savoring it like the finest of wines. As long as blood courses through my veins, and thoughts flow through my mind, my soul will dance with joy, and my heart will sing with love.

I am one of the 7% of the living, and I am grateful."

Chapter Three

How to Live Like a Champion

Would you like to live like a champion—someone who regularly wins in life? Would you like to consistently achieve the best results in your relationships, finances, health, and mental well-being?

Now you can by following four simple steps:

Step One: Avoid the Little Bads

We may not realize it, but we often say negative phrases to ourselves— "little bads"—that become a part of our psychological makeup: "I don't have enough time." "I don't have enough money." "Life is difficult." "I can't find someone to love."

These small, pocket-sized samples of negativity become ingrained in our minds, and before we know it, we start to feel bad, negative, and drained of energy.

The key to defeat the "little bads" is to transform them into "little goods"—simple words of encouragement and positivity that you repeat to yourself in your daily thoughts. You say to yourself, "I have all the time I need," "There is an abundance of money and love," and "Life, with positive belief, is easy."

In the beginning, the "little bads" will give you resistance. After all, they have lived in your mind for a long time—sometimes from as early as your childhood. They don't want to lose their place of power in your life, and they will fight you to remain in the darkest crevices of your mind. To defeat them, you need consistency. Every day, practice repeating the "little goods" so that you start to believe them—more and more. Over time, these pockets of positivity will multiply and outnumber the "little bads"—eventually becoming ingrained in your mind and taking the place of the old negative and self-defeating thoughts.

As you begin to speak differently to yourself, your attitude will brighten, and you will have far more energy, motivation, and desire to accomplish your goals.

Step Two: Start with the Easy

Many times, we may want to do something in life—start a new career, relationship, or lifestyle—but we think doing so will be too hard. We fear it will require too much effort. The solution is to begin with an easy step. Do something you can complete in a short period of time without much effort.

If, for example, you want to start a new career, go online and read a couple of articles about people who have been successful in that field.

If you want to write a book, start with the first sentence, with the first idea—just write down the first few phrases that come to your mind.

If you want to get in shape, decide that you're going to go to the gym for only 20 minutes the first time.

As you take these small steps—in psychology they are called successive approximations to the goal—you begin to build momentum to take bigger steps and accomplish bigger goals. You build on the earlier successes for future successes.

The online search leads you to a mentor you can learn from. The early sentences lead to more writing and longer paragraphs. The 20 minutes at the gym become 30, then 45, then one hour, and you start to see the results in your physique and physical health—which motivate you to work out even more.

Pablo was a shy social worker in his mid-20s who was grossly overweight. Tipping the scales at nearly 400 pounds, he knew he had to lose weight—for his health and social confidence. He felt unattractive to women and had never dated much; he had always been a chubby kid with low self-esteem.

After reading about the concept of Start with the Easy, and talking it over with his mother, Pablo decided to make some small, but simple, changes in his lifestyle. He began by cutting out fatty foods from his diet while reducing his carbohydrate intake (tortillas, rice, and bread). At the same time, he started walking around his neighborhood—first one block, then two blocks. He also checked out some gyms online and decided to visit one. Initially, he was too embarrassed to walk into the gym feeling "so fat." But the gym manager treated him with kindness and respect, and started him on a basic exercise plan with a trainer.

Gradually, Pablo began to lose weight, eat healthier, and interact more with people, including women. After losing 100 pounds, and gaining a new sense of confidence, Pablo knows he is on the right track. He is starting to believe that he can accomplish whatever he sets his mind to do.

Like Pablo, you can start with the easy. The first early, easy steps toward your goal will lead you toward living like a champion and having a higher level of accomplishment that further propels you forward. Soon, your momentum will carry you toward accomplishing those goals that, at first, seemed difficult or impossible. You are on your way.

Step Three: Practice the Power of Discard

People who live like champions speed confidently forward, not by acquiring something, but by first discarding what they don't need. They realize that what often holds them back are things they are accumulating that don't serve a valuable purpose, such as unrealistic beliefs and negative expectations.

To transform your life, begin to discard the negative thoughts that hold you back: That you're not smart or capable enough to obtain the career or financial security you want; that you're not lovable enough to find the love you desire.

Tell yourself the opposite: You are smart, lovable, and successful. You will achieve the relationship you desire; the career or financial success you really want. Each day, focus on replacing Self-Defeating thoughts with life-affirming Invincible thoughts until Invincibility reigns within you.

Although refuting your negative thoughts is an effective approach to self-power, some may argue that this is easier said than done. They say, "I have tried to eliminate negative thoughts for a long time, but they still keep coming back." It is true—Self-defeating thoughts often return because they have grown comfortable in your mind; they make you think that you need them; that you would be lonely and lost without them.

What you need to do is make these destructive thought forces uncomfortable by changing up your normal routines and psychological patterns. One way to accomplish this is to start a parallel process— you will eliminate junk from your outside world at the same time that you eliminate "inner trash"— negative, self-defeating thoughts—from your mind.

You will start by discarding old items and junk from your home— personal items you no longer use; objects you no longer look at, or think about. These are the items that are not important parts of your past, or treasured mementos, but simply accumulated items that are no longer of much value: old clothes that no longer fit, equipment that doesn't work well, paperwork that is obsolete.

When you discard external junk from your life, you will say to yourself, "I am eliminating all that is not useful, healthy, or productive— including useless physical items, as well as old self-destructive thought patterns that used to scare and control me." As you do this, your house will not only be cleaner and more organized, but you will also reduce the number of self-destructive thoughts in your mind. Your thinking process will become more clear, refreshed, and focused. The external simplicity you experience will begin to translate into internal simplicity and freedom from nagging negativities. Soon, you will begin to attract the things you really need such as transforming beliefs, accurate judgments, and fruitful actions.

Step Four: Join a Mastermind Group

The last phase of living like a champion is to join or create a Mastermind Group. This is a union of like-minded people who have a certain expertise—perhaps, in psychology, business, science, art, home improvement, and so on. These individuals meet regularly (weekly or monthly) to exchange ideas, support each other, and help solve mutual problems.

If, for example, you want to start a business, find three or four of the best business-minded people you know and get together regularly for coffee or lunch. Bring your notepad or tablet and let the ideas flow.

In the first stage of idea gathering, the rule is that no one in the group will critique the ideas that are presented. The first phase of the group process is solely to generate ideas—as many as possible. This is known as the "hot phase" as participants come up with fresh ideas quickly and passionately—generating a great deal of excitement in the process.

Later, in the cooling stage, mastermind members calmly and patiently analyze and critique the ideas. They discard the weaker ones while keeping and developing the best ones.

This Mastermind process can work well for any topic you are interested in, whether it's raising children, being a good cook, or inventing something to make a positive contribution to the world.

The important ingredient of the Mastermind Group is that you regularly meet with like-minded people who share your values and vision, and who sincerely want to help you reach your greatest goals as you help them reach theirs.

What if you're shy or Introverted? You say it's hard for you to meet people or approach others who hold value for you. The key is to reverse your thinking and realize that you can give your mastermind partner(s) as much, if not more, value than they give you. You can help them by offering your own insights, personality, and thought process. Eventually, that value will be returned to you in the form of new ideas, valuable contacts, and life-changing inspirations from those in your Mastermind Group. Start today and get involved in online and offline groups that resonate with your interests so you can meet like-minded people who will form your first mastermind group. The more energy and mind power you can harness with positive and life-affirming individuals, the more effective and impactful your Mastermind Group will be.

To summarize, here are the four steps to Live Like a Champion:

1. **Avoid the Little Bads**: Build up a storehouse of positivity and strong, success-producing thoughts in place of the defeating and nagging little negative thoughts.
2. **Start with the Easy**: Begin with what you can do with little effort. Generate momentum, a strong flow of energy and power, that leads you directly to achieving your ultimate goals.
3. **Practice the Power of Discard**: Throw away all things, both objects and thought patterns, that no longer have value for you. Clean out your garage, throw away old items, and get rid of faulty thinking ("I am no good for…."). When you get rid of what doesn't work, you will be one step closer to what does work for you: your Invincible Mind.
4. **Join a Mastermind Group**: Unite yourself with like-minded people in a weekly or monthly group in which you come up with fresh ideas to help each other reach important goals.

By applying these four strategies in your life, you will not only begin to Live Like a Champion, but you will also be one step closer to a marvelous life of Invincibility and impeccable excellence.

Chapter Four

The Three Tries—Your Roadmap to Excellence

Would you like to achieve your greatest goals in life and live your heart's desires? You can if you apply the principle of the Three Tries to your life: Trying in the right way to achieve your goals.

When we were little kids, we were told to try hard. Our parents told us that the harder we try, the better results we will have in our grades, hobbies, sports activities, and eventually, in grown-up jobs. Although they meant well, our parents were only half right. Psychology tells us that trying too hard can actually defeat our purpose. If we do more of the wrong things, we tend to get more of the same bad results. Also, the anxiety that comes from trying too hard can actually impede our progress—we are distracted from doing the things that will actually lead to our happiness and success.

According to a study published in the *Journal of Social and Clinical Psychology*, seeking happiness too intently can actually lead to depression (Ford, Shallcross, Mauss, Floerke, and Gruber, 2014). By monitoring their ability to attain happiness, individuals may actually impair their happiness—they become so self-conscious about trying to be happy that they reduce their happiness in the process.

When we think about effort, we can examine the word, "conation," which refers to any natural tendency, impulse, or directed effort. Conation has to do with your intent and desire to do something. In other words, how you "try" in life to make an impact. Depending on how you try, you will get good results or bad results. If you try to quit smoking, but hang around smokers, you may have a hard time quitting. On the other hand, if you associate with people who value a healthy lifestyle that incorporates diet and exercise, you will have a much better chance of quitting smoking.

There is a superior way to achieve your goals and dreams. It is called "Effective Trying," and consists of putting forth the right effort, in the right way, for the right goals. When you follow the Effective Trying methods described below, you will have an accurate roadmap to your ultimate success and happiness.

Let's take a look at three examples of Ineffective Trying, and three ways to accomplish Effective Trying.

Ineffective Trying #1: Not Trying at All

Many times, we give up when we don't achieve our goals. We try for that ideal career, relationship, or mental attitude, but we keep failing. Eventually, we give up; we stop trying.

In psychology, this is known as learned helplessness. In rat experiments, some rats were given electric shocks they couldn't escape from (Seligman & Beagley, 1975). They were later placed in a box with a lever that would allow them to escape the shocks. The rats who were initially given inescapable shocks did not attempt to escape the box by pressing the lever—even though there were no more shocks for them. They had learned to be helpless.

It applies to humans, too. At some point after having a few failures in trying to achieve our goals, we believe we can't succeed. We stop trying to avoid the pain of failing. We give up; we have "learned" to be helpless.

The Effective Trying Solution:
Meditate on Greatness

Meditating on greatness is the antidote to giving up too soon. Meditating on greatness means that you study and reflect on the lives of people who have already achieved what you desire.

If you want a great relationship, study people who have them. If you want to make more money, find a financial mentor who can teach you the ropes of finances. If you want spiritual peace, learn from someone who truly has it.

Ever since she was a child, Heather, a human resources specialist in her late-20s, had wanted to make a difference in the world. A sociology student in college, she had graduated and started working in Human Resources, but she wasn't happy. She wanted to make a bigger impact on the world and found herself drawn to politics.

Encouraged by a friend who had worked for a political campaign, she made contact with one of the women she admired: a local congresswoman who was a strong advocate for women and children. Summoning up her courage, she arranged a meeting and was inspired by the congresswoman's zeal and commitment to equality and fair treatment for the disadvantaged.

Deciding to volunteer for the congresswoman's campaign, Heather enjoyed her work tremendously and decided that she was a natural at politics and campaigning for higher principles. She learned a great deal under the mentorship of the congresswoman, and is now redirecting her career focus.

Her new plan: To earn her Master's Degree in Public Administration in an online program as she prepares for her new career in public service. She is so excited that she can hardly contain her enthusiasm for her new vocation in life: making a real difference in the world.

You can follow Heather's example and absorb the knowledge and wisdom of those who have already succeeded in the area you are interested in. When you do this, you have a road map to avoid the electric shocks (pain) of the world. You can go through the maze of life accomplishing your goals with minimum pain and maximum satisfaction.

In your search for a mentor, you may be hesitant to approach them at first. Perhaps, you think, "They are too important or busy to be interested in talking to me." Although some successful people are self-important and don't want to take time to help others, there are plenty more who experience great pleasure in mentoring individuals who are eager to learn. They realize that they owe a lot of their success to the help they received from others, and they feel a psychological and spiritual calling to pass along their wisdom and experience to those who are striving for excellence.

Go ahead and make that call, send an email, text, or message, write a letter. Tell them what you admire about their lives; express how much their work has impacted your life for the better. Tell them what you will do with the knowledge you receive from them—explore a new career, business, or relationship; make a lifestyle change, help others in a unique way. When you approach them with a sincere desire to learn and contribute, you may be surprised at how willing and open your success mentor is to helping you.

Another important point: When picking a role model or mentor, be sure that they actually walk the path they're talking about. There are so-called experts or gurus who talk a good game, but don't actually live up to the words they are saying. You want to evaluate the advice-givers by their results. Are they successful in accomplishing what they truly want? Are they content with themselves after they get what they want? Do they really have peace and happiness?

If they live by their words, then listen to their advice while maintaining your own mindset and integrity—incorporating the parts of them that resonate with the essence of you.

Ineffective Trying Example #2:
Trying Too Hard

Another problem we have is trying too hard. When you try too hard, you often end up having the opposite effect: You push away the very thing you are chasing.

Have you ever noticed the man or woman who tries too hard to impress a potential romantic partner, while secretly believing that he or she is inadequate or unworthy? The end result is that they end up pushing their romantic interest away. The desired person will likely feel pressured and suffocated from all the attention they are receiving from the needy person.

Why do we try so hard? One reason is that, deep down, we don't believe we are good enough to achieve what we want. We believe in the "little bads" that tell us we don't deserve to be successful and happy—to have that great relationship, career, lifestyle, or psychological peace of mind. So, we try to overcompensate by trying too hard, rushing too much, worrying excessively—even though we know, deep down, that we often push away the very things we desire when we push too much.

There's a better way to exert effort to achieve your goals. It is called Reverse Your Trying.

The Effective Trying Solution:
Reverse Your Trying

When you Reverse Your Trying, you intentionally do the opposite of what you have been trying to do. Instead of trying harder, you will relax and flow with life circumstances.

Let's say, for example, that you have been exerting a lot of effort to find a soul mate or love partner, and you have been frustrated in the process. The person you desire doesn't want you, while the ones you don't want are interested in you.

At this point, you will do the opposite of what you've been doing: Take a temporary break from dating and enjoy being by yourself for a while. You can pick up a hobby, make new friends, travel, adopt a pet, start a new spiritual practice or exercise regimen, or take some classes. Now, instead of mentally chasing other people, you will focus on developing a sense of peace and contentment—as you relax and wait for the right person to come into your life.

Of course, pulling back from your goals isn't always easy to do, especially if you think of yourself as a "go-getter"—a hard-driving person who feels like a failure if you take "no" for an answer. You may believe that you are "lazy" or "weak" if you don't try with all of your might to achieve your objectives.

In reality, you are stronger and more powerful when you occasionally pull back from your overstrenuous effort to achieve your goals. When you're able to stop trying so hard (when you're not getting the results you want), you are exercising patience and manifesting strength of mind to wait for the good things to come your way. Although you still maintain a strong view on what you desire, your primary focus is on your inner development first—becoming the most Invincible person you can possibly be—which, in turn, will help you achieve both inner and outer excellence.

For example, instead of trying to meet a quality person for a relationship, you will focus on becoming a quality person— being patient, compassionate, and forgiving; helping others and contributing to make the world a more peaceful and harmonious place. In the process, you will expand yourself—your core nature, your inner traits—so you become your best self. When you do this, your confidence rises. As your best self, you will also be more attractive and genuine, and you will naturally attract the person who resonates with who you really are.

The beauty of reverse trying is that you liberate yourself from the tension and fear that normally accompany trying too hard—you take things in a more relaxed and accepting way. As a result, you are able to think more clearly, act more decisively, and achieve better results.

Ineffective Trying Example #3:
Trying for the Wrong Things

Now we get to one of the biggest problems in society: trying for goals that do not fulfill us, while ignoring the things that are truly good for us. An artist strives to make more money even though that is not his primary passion in life. A businesswoman is told by friends to relax more and lie on the beach, even though making money is her greatest talent (she loves it), and she hates wasting time.

There is nothing wrong with either money or relaxation. What matters is whether a goal matches who you really are inside. If a businessperson enjoys making money in a way that contributes to society, then that is an appropriate goal for that person. If another person has a passion for the arts and loves to create things, then pursuing artistic creation is the ideal objective for them.

On the other hand, when a person has mismatched goals, they don't act from their true nature or inclinations. They end up suffering because they expend too much energy chasing the wrong things— objectives that can never truly satisfy them.

The Effective Trying Solution: Try for
Your Don—Your God-Given Talent

The answer to trying for the wrong things is to focus on goals that are a fit for your natural, God-given (nature-given) ability.

This natural ability is known as a "Don," and comes from the Spanish word for "gift" or "talent" ("Don Divino" means gift from God). A Don is a secret wellspring of ability, power, and skill that is unique to your psychological DNA. This special ability—also called "multiple intelligences," "strengths," or "talents"—is a reservoir of inner power and ability that represents your birthright. You were born with this talent and can use it to improve your life and the lives of others.

Your talent can be emotional, spiritual, financial, athletic, scientific, artistic, nurturing, or word-related. You may have one main talent, or you may have more than one. Usually, one or two of your talents will be the strongest, and that is what you should perfect to your fullest capacity.

How do you discover your Don? Ask yourself, "What do I love to do for fun even if I'm not being paid for it?" Then, ask yourself: "Am I good at this, or can I become better at it?" Finally, ask yourself, "Do I want to do this for a hobby or for a living?"

For example, let's say that you love cooking, and you are good at it. You cook for your friends and family, but you decide that you don't want to make money from your talent; you want to do it as a labor of love for those you care about. In addition, you enjoy working with computers. Although you are not an expert at working with them yet, you would like to learn more, and you believe you can make money from your computer skills to help support your family.

Regardless of what your "Don" is, your mission is to actualize that ability for the greater good of others—which is then naturally reflected back to you in your own inner growth and happiness. Of course, it's perfectly fine for the businessperson to dabble in leisure, or for the artist to learn about finances. Yet, the key to your happiness and success is to develop the true power or ability you have inside—the wonderful talent called "Don."

When you put all of your effort into your Don, you will see positive results in many areas of your life—your relationships, finances, career, health, and happiness. You will find that you can accomplish more in less time—success comes easier for you—because you are tapping into your natural strengths instead of trying to force things that you're not good at.

On the other hand, when you don't live from your Don, you will achieve less—you will be more tired because nothing moves you deeply. You lack energy because you go through the motions by doing things that don't truly motivate and inspire you.

Things are different when your life revolves around expressing your Don, your innate talent and greatest ability. When you do that, you will have boundless energy. You will be strongly motivated because you know you are doing the thing you love to do. As you experience more success in life by sharing your Don with the world, your confidence and ability will grow. You will be able to do more because you have become more.

Your goal is to have a profound connection—to be absolutely enthralled—with something that relates to your Don; whether it's a creative project, a cause, or helping the people you love. Throw yourself into your Don with complete abandon, and you will achieve results like never before.

The Go For It Principle: Your Jumpstart to Excellence

Expressing our Don can build motivation and confidence, but sometimes we hold ourselves back from using our talents and achieving our life dreams because we doubt our abilities. We don't believe we are good enough; we fear we will be rejected or fail.

The solution to this problem is known as the "Go For It" principle: Go for what you truly want in life, even though you're not sure you will get it. Working towards what you truly desire, even if you don't fully achieve it on your first efforts, is the very action that opens the doors to tremendous success in your life.

For example, let's say you have a fear of public speaking. At the same time, you recognize how speaking can help your career and earning potential, and how it can give you social confidence. As a result, you decide to confront your fear and speak in public. In your first speaking engagement, you are very nervous, but you do OK—nobody laughs you off the stage.

The next time, you focus on the one person in the audience who is responding well to you, the individual who is nodding their head and smiling. Suddenly, you feel more confident; your speech goes much better. Gradually, the more you participate in public speaking, and master the fear behind it, the more you will be confident and relaxed. Eventually, public speaking may even become a favorite activity for you because you have broken through the fear barrier to do what you wanted to do.

When you make a sincere effort toward achieving what you desire, you momentarily interrupt the fear mechanism—the fear that you will fail—that has kept you from achieving your goal. You will take a step forward when you move toward your objective with strong intention, even if you don't succeed at first. In this way, you have imprinted a new message in your mind that bypasses the fear.

This new thought tells you: "I will strive for what I want despite the fear." You are encouraged to keep pursuing your dream despite the possibility of failure and rejection. Whether you succeed or fail momentarily doesn't really matter. You may not get what you desire initially, but you have done wonders for your self-confidence anyway. You have broken through the fear barrier. That is more valuable than gold.

If you do the thing you fear, your image of yourself will be upgraded. You will create in your mind the image of the person you want to be: confidently assured, competent, and calm. By deliberately doing something that is causing you fear, you begin to break the hold that fear has over you. The more you take a step toward your desires, despite the fear, the easier it will be for you to drive out doubts and feelings of inadequacy.

Here's a simple truth: When you really live as you like, and go for what you truly desire, you will be genuinely happy. You will bypass the limitations of fear, and you will no longer be enslaved by false expectations of what it means to live your life. You no longer have to be perfect, or act in a certain way, to please other people. You can simply be yourself and that is enough.

Now your efforts will be rewarded. You will try for what you want, and you will achieve it. Neither fear nor failure will have a hold over you. You are free to be your True nature, which is all you need to be the happiest and most successful person you can possibly be.

The Three Tries: Your Route to Ultimate Success

Achieving your goals is much easier when you focus your energy on the things that truly matter. Here is a recap of what you need to do:

1. **Meditate on Greatness**: Study and follow the examples of those who have made it where you want to go—inspiration and motivation will surely follow. By absorbing the best lessons of others who have gone before, you will blaze your own trail to greatness.

2. **Reverse Your Trying**: Do the opposite of what you've been doing, and you will receive the opposite of what you've been getting. When you think outside of your usual ways, your results will be greater because you see things from a different perspective.

3. **Try for Your Don**: Focus on expressing your God-given, natural talent. You will be happier and more successful when you tap into your unique abilities to achieve your dreams. There is nothing better than doing what is uniquely you.

Soon, you will no longer be trying, but you will be doing and succeeding—your intention will become reality because you are on your own side.

Nothing will be able to stop you.

Chapter Five

It's Never Too Late to Win Big

I often hear these words when the topic of self-change and self-improvement come up among my clients and students: "It's too late for me. I've made too many mistakes in life. I can't change my circumstances."

If you believe that, then I have some good news for you:

It's never too late.

You may say that you have made too many mistakes; that you are too far down in life to ever get off the ground. You might say you're a drug or alcohol addict; you might say you've been stuck so many years in the wrong relationship or job. You may argue that you have done too many wrong and shameful things in your life; you have hurt too many people. Most of all, you have hurt yourself and wasted your potential. You can never recapture the time you lost; you have lost the game.

Here is something that is going to change your thinking if you truly believe it:

No matter how far you have fallen down into the well of despair, you can still look up and see the sun shine. You can still see the hope of life, even from where you are, right now, at this very moment.

It's never too late.

"It's never too late" means that it doesn't matter how old you are. You can still have a happy and successful life—regardless of how many disappointments and frustrations you have experienced.

Research in brain plasticity shows us that we can emotionally rewire our brains even as we get older. According to a study cited in the *Journal of Psychology*, it was found that changes in brain chemistry, architecture, and performance are associated with lifestyle choices such as maintaining a positive outlook (Shaffer, 2012).

Yes, it's true: Even if you're older, or have failed before, you can still rewire your brain by adding more positive thoughts and emotions into your life on a daily basis. It doesn't matter how many times you have to strike a match before it ignites; once it ignites, the fire will burn.

It's time now to ignite the fire of your Invincible Mind. You can change your life with a new set of behaviors that will help you grow your positivity muscles—your ability to be positive and helpful to yourself and others on a daily basis, despite the circumstances. Just like you exercise your physical muscles, you can also increase your ability to be confident and optimistic in the face of adversity and negative people and situations.

Begin today. Smile, pay a stranger a compliment, help an elderly person with their groceries, count your blessings, meditate while imagining that you are spreading loving kindness to your community. Although these may seem like simple actions that some of us do anyway, the key is to have conscious awareness that you are expressing kindness and positivity outwardly to others. By doing these simple acts of love extension—extending a positive and life-affirming energy to others— you start to make inner changes in your brain circuitry. You think in more positive ways; you feel grateful that you can help others, which in turn, increases your self-confidence and belief that you are a positive influence in this world.

Many people, unfortunately, feel like imposters in their lives. They try to be good and kind and nice, but they also realize how petty, selfish, impatient, and angry they can be inside their own minds. This disparity causes them to experience pain and makes them feel like they are not worthy of love and joy. As a result, they project their inner sense of unworthiness outward onto the world, and the world returns the favor in the form of broken relationships, missed opportunities, and a general sense of dissatisfaction and deprivation. This, in turn, makes them feel even more angry and frustrated at how the world and other people have treated them. Eventually, they may even give up on love, on life, on happiness.

The good news is that there is another part of your mind—the Invincible Mind—that is positive, life-affirming, and powerful. This part is full of compassion, gratitude, love, confidence, and goodwill. Although it may be small in the beginning of your Invincible journey, it can grow in power. By releasing your loving energy outwardly to others and the world, you begin the express the hidden elements of your Invincibility that have been covered up until now, as you bring more creativity, energy, resilience, longevity, and happiness into your life. Soon, you will be on your way toward your true state of mind: Invincibility.

To be Invincible means that you are able to defeat outside enemies or circumstances, as well as the negativities in your own mind. At its essence, Invincibility is a state of continual elevation and freedom in which you're free of adverse thoughts and emotions.

When you are psychologically Invincible in the way we are describing, you are confident, loving, and successful.

Sadly, many of us are our own worst enemies when it comes to infecting our minds with negative thoughts—otherwise known as Self-Defeating Thoughts. These Self-Defeating Thoughts are always interfering with our happiness and productivity.

In your mind, you may have created self-condemning thoughts such as "I'm not....good enough, smart enough, attractive enough, etc.... to succeed in life." "I am doomed to failure." "I can't win."

With Invincibility thinking, you start to reverse the old negativities and learn how to harness those maladaptive inner voices for your own use and power. Best of all, you can begin to create positive mental forces, also known as Invincible Thoughts.

The simple truth is that, no matter how much you have suffered or lost in the past, you can still create a mind full of positive thought forces. You can have Invincibility right now. You can have both mental and environmental mastery; you can live with passion, purpose, and power.

Here are some simple rules to implement as you develop your Invincibility:

Rule Number One: Transform Your Pain into Power

The first step is to recognize that everything you have called "pain" in your past is simply an energy stimulus—something that evokes a reaction. What happened to you in the past is simply leftover energy, an old mental imprint, that you can transmute (or change) to help your personal growth and advancement. You can take the energy that you used to call "pain" and turn it into an unstoppable force for good, growth, and healing.

Jerome, a business consultant in his late-40s, was a hard-working man with a beautiful family. The problem was that he worked too much; some would call him a workaholic—working at least 70 to 80 hours per week. He had made some good investments, and had provided financial security for his family, but he felt driven to make even more money and have more success.

Then, everything changed. On a rainy night, he was coming home late from work, when suddenly he was rear-ended by a semi-truck. Jerome suffered devastating injuries, including broken bones in his arms and legs, and was bedridden after being released from the hospital. Frustrated and angry that he couldn't work, he plunged into a deep depression. He didn't want to talk to anyone. He didn't want to do anything; he didn't even feel like shaving. Most of the time, he just lay in bed watching TV.

Now that he was home all of the time, his family took the opportunity to shower him with laughter, love, and fun.

Although he was resistant at first to their good cheer, he gradually started to bask in their love and affection. His depression began to lift; he started to smile and laugh again.

One night, he was reading a book to his nine-year-old daughter as she and the family dog lay next to him, and he realized how much he loved his family and enjoyed being with them. He clearly saw how it took a near deadly accident for him to realize what he had been missing.

After he recovered months later, Jerome still worked hard, but he made sure to spend more quality time with his family—even turning down extra work to have more time with them. He had learned an important lesson: All the money in the world doesn't mean a thing if you don't have something to live for: family and love.

Like Jerome, you can learn how to transform your pain into power— to apply the lessons learned from mistakes and obstacles to initiate a fresh beginning in your life. In this way, you can take the energy that you used to call "pain" or "defeat" and turn it into an unstoppable force for good, growth, and healing.

For example, let's say that you had a setback in your career or business. You lost a job or your business went bankrupt. As a consequence, you may fall into sadness or depression—a dark and gloomy state in which you don't want to do anything; you just want to stay home and sleep.

Although this depressed state is painful, you can also consider it to be a quiet and reflective time that you can use as a form of meditative guidance. Since depression has slowed down your mental movements, you have time to reflect on what really matters to you. You can go deeper into your thoughts and feelings, perhaps with the help of a good coach or therapist, and you can learn about what you really want in life—what you need to do to move towards your deepest desires.

When you are feeling sad or down, here is an exercise you can do to transform your sadness into joy:

Exercise: Imagine Your Best Future

Find a comfortable and private place; perhaps in your room, backyard, or somewhere in nature. Sit quietly with your eyes closed. Inhale deeply through your nose; exhale through your mouth.

Now imagine what your ideal future would be like 5 years, 10 years, and even 15 years from today if you obtain what you want in your career, relationships, and life experiences. Take another deep breath and visualize what you will look like, what you will be doing, where you will be, who will be around you, and how you will be feeling in this ideal future.

When you open your eyes, write down what you experienced and felt in this ideal future. Perhaps, you see yourself with a loving partner and family, doing the work you love, and spending time with the people you care about. You see yourself as being attractive, successful, healthy, and happy in this ideal future.

With this exercise, you will be able to transform your past by mentally creating a future of excellence. With so much to look forward to, you will no longer be bound by the pain and regret of the past—the painful past will lose its hold over your thoughts and feelings because your future is now.

Rule Number Two: Learn from the Greats Who Overcame Adversity

No matter how low you have sunk in life—in your finances, personal habits, or self-confidence—you can still harness that amazing power of focus and motivation. You can do this by studying the noble examples of those special individuals who have triumphed over great adversity. They include:

Marla Runyan: The first blind athlete to qualify for the US Olympic team. She also earned her Master's Degree in Special Education and taught blind children in schools.

Stephen Hawking: A prolific scientist and author who lost his ability to speak or move due to ALS disease and did groundbreaking work in physics and cosmology.

Malala Yousafzai: A Pakistani woman who was shot in the head by a political group and became a global advocate for human rights, women's rights, and the right to education. At the age of 17, she became the youngest Nobel Peace prize winner (co-recipient of the 2014 Nobel Peace Prize).

Nick Vujicic: Born with no arms and no legs due to an extremely rare congenital disease, he became an internationally recognized author, motivational speaker, and evangelist. Married to a lovely, able-bodied woman, he had four beautiful, healthy children, and shared his inspirational story around the world.

You can learn from achievers who have overcome great obstacles by reading their books, listening to their podcasts and videos, and gaining wisdom from their lives. By modeling their unrelenting dedication to a higher cause despite problems and setbacks, you will be able to reenact their excellence and contentment while experiencing it in your own way.

There are many stories of influential and productive people who have started later in life; resilient individuals who have overcome pain and failure to leave a lasting legacy. Find an individual who resonates with you—an esteemed figure who has been successful at doing something you're interested in. Study their lives. If they are historical figures, read their books and watch videos about them. If they are alive, contact them personally and see if you can interact with them by email, phone, or in person.

If, for example, you love the world of finance, find an investment specialist or renowned money expert with whom you can discuss market trends and portfolios.

If you're into art, look up an artist you admire and study their work—go to their exhibits.

If you want to be a great parent, have lunch with a mature couple who have successfully raised children and grandchildren. If they are also happy in their marriage after many years, you will want to learn their secrets. Interview them as if you're writing a blog and ask them about their keys to marital bliss and successful parenthood.

Regardless of what type of field or expertise you want to explore, remember that experts often like to pass along their knowledge and wisdom to help the next generation. If you make an attempt to connect with them, chances are you will receive a positive response from one of your admirable teachers, and they will want to help you. By applying their wisdom in your life, you can begin to progress and overcome any obstacles that stand in your way.

Rule Number Three: Keep Walking Forward

When you get discouraged about "taking a step backward" into your old bad habits and self-defeating thinking, consider this:

If you take two steps forward, and one step backward, *you are still making progress.* If your overall movement is forward, you are still getting to where you want to be.

Many times, we are too hard on ourselves for our mistakes. We chastise ourselves about not being able to change our negative habits; about getting caught up with the same harmful people.

Stop right now. Recognize that you are walking forward despite your mistakes. You are on the right path to Invincibility.

As you walk forward toward your inner growth, you may have a combination of excitement and trepidation. Part of your mind is eager to live a happier and healthier life and wants to move forward; another part (Self-Defeating) may be skeptical and doubtful.

This Self-Defeating part of your mind doubts that you have the willpower or dedication to work on yourself. It tells you to postpone your inner work because it will be too hard. As your doubts increase, it warns you: "Let's wait until you are ready to start making changes in your life. Things are too stressful now; you don't have the energy and strength to do anything big. Let's wait until…the kids are grown up, you save more money, you are ready psychologically to make a move."

On and on, the Self-Defeating Mind will tell you to wait, postpone, and procrastinate. That is the wrong advice. If you wait until tomorrow to make a positive change in your life, tomorrow will never come because there will always be another reason, another excuse, for not taking positive action—most of which revolve around the fear of rejection or failure.

When should you start increasing your personal power and emotional strength?

The answer is simple: Start Now.

It is never too late to make a positive change in your life. Begin today to raise your level of emotional and psychological power, so you can make an improvement in your state of mind—even a small one at first.

In fact, one small step in your favor, in the direction of your Invincibility, is another step away from your past follies, regrets, and embarrassments.

The more you walk toward your own Invincibility, the more wonders you will see. It may seem difficult or challenging at first, but you will see that the path becomes easier the more steps you take toward your inner development.

Your Invincible Mind education is like riding a bicycle for the first time. In the beginning, you may have fallen down a few times, but eventually bike riding became an automatic and enjoyable process for you. You grew into the bicycle and it became natural for you. In the same way, you will grow into becoming an Invincible person; it will become natural for you.

You will grow every time you work on yourself by reading a self-help book, attending a personal development lecture, or listening to a transformational CD or podcast. You will make progress whenever you practice the principles you are learning here.

Before long, you will realize that you are winning big: You are reaching the state of Invincibility in which nothing can harm or bother you. Success is your every step.

How do you know when you are winning big? When you no longer think about success and happiness; when you *are* success and happiness. It's like this: When a sea creature lives in the ocean, it doesn't need to worry about a lack of water; it has everything it needs.

Be a person who lives in your own psychological ocean: You are an Invincible person who has everything you need to live with total freedom, creativity, and love. Make your life bigger each day until it is so big that nothing can stop you.

Always remember that it's never too late to win big and live joyfully. Keep these steps in mind as you master challenges in life and reach your highest potential:

1. **Transform Your Pain into Power**
2. **Learn From the Greats Who Overcame Adversity**
3. **Keep Walking Forward**

PART TWO

JOURNEY TOWARD INVINCIBILITY

Chapter Six

....

Master the Desert of Weakness

Did you know that your worst weakness can become your greatest strength?

If you know how to do it, you can transform your weaknesses and faults into amazing strengths and attributes. By doing so, you will work wonders in your life and live to your fullest potential. You no longer have to be afraid of the things that used to hold you back; you can tap into their hidden power and use them for your own good.

It starts by understanding how your mind works. In your mind, you have two locations for your thoughts: A Mountain of Invincibility and a Desert of Weakness.

A mountain is a large natural elevation of the earth's surface that gives you a superior vantagepoint. Because your perspective is from a higher place, you have a clear view—you can see a far distance. At the same time, the air you breathe on the mountaintop is fresh and clean and there is plenty of water.

In a similar way, the Mountain of Invincibility is the part of your mind that is elevated, refreshing, and secure. It holds positive thoughts, including creativity, compassion, confidence, gratitude, gentleness, patience, and love. This is where you draw sustenance for daily challenges; where you generate your momentum, enthusiasm, and persistence. As you climb the mountain of your own mind, you will surpass obstacles and setbacks, and you will get to the top of your true potential.

From the Mountain of Invincibility, you can see life from a different perspective; the things that used to bother you now seem small to you. You are able to see the big picture of your greatness. When you reside on the Mountain of Invincibility, no problem or challenge seems too big; you feel you can overcome anything. In this safe and secure mental place, you have no fear or psychological limits. Your confidence is strong; your faith is unshakeable.

On the other hand, the Desert of Weakness is the holding place for all of the negative, critical, and self-attacking thoughts that have built up inside your mind over the years.

In the physical world, a desert is a place that is hot and dry and drains the energy and life of those who are unfortunate enough to be stranded there. The wanderer's throat is parched as they chase after mirages (optical illusions), seeking water to quench their overwhelming thirst.

Mentally, the Desert of Weakness is an ugly place devoid of nourishment—projecting a "mental mirage" in which you try to seek comfort and satisfaction from your own thoughts, only to find that these same thoughts turn against you; tormenting you with the pain and emptiness of resentments, fears, anger, sadness, frustration, and futility. In this psychological nightmare, you are trapped by bad habits and compulsions; by perceived inadequacies and self-demeaning thoughts and feelings.

The Desert of Weakness is an expert at tormenting you with harmful and critical voices from your past:

"You're not smart enough."
"You're not attractive enough."
"You're not lovable enough."
"You're not confident enough."
"You're not financially successful enough."

The Desert of Weakness knows your weak points. It knows the inner mental places where it can apply the most pressure. It knows how to make you backslide into your old habits and bad decisions. It thrives on tormenting you with your weakness—by reminding you of your past inadequacies and failures.

It attacks you:

"Just take one more bite of that chocolate ice cream. It won't hurt your diet."

"Call him again. So, what if he's a little crazy? He's too irresistible."

"You're terrible at finances; don't even think of investing. You'll lose it all."

Clever and relentless, the Desert of Weakness likes to utilize Self-Defeating thoughts to attack and keep you weak so you don't have enough willpower to move toward the side of Invincibility.

The ultimate goal of the Desert of Weakness is to encourage you to indulge in negative and self-critical thoughts: "I can never get ahead financially"; "I can never lose weight"; "I can never find true love." These thoughts, in turn, create a pressure in you to relieve the negative feelings from the thoughts by engaging in self-harming actions: excessive spending for a luxury item, eating and drinking too much, getting involved in harmful and toxic relationships.

To escape the pain from the thought, you may behave rashly. However, this creates another pressure: You feel ashamed and inadequate, which creates another cycle of self-condemnation, followed by more self-damaging actions: more expensive, but unnecessary purchases, more overeating and excessive drinking, rebounding into another negative relationship.

The problem is that your self-defeating mindset remains unchanged between the two acts; the second act—falling back into the old self-harming habits—is also the outcome of the same negative mindset. Because you felt regretful and guilty, you didn't have the willpower to change your behavior: to stick to your budget, go on a diet, or leave the bad relationship.

Consequently, you fall into a vicious cycle of negative actions followed by negative feelings—prompting you to repeat the same bad actions because you don't feel you can do any better. When you think of the mistakes you have made in the past, you feel weak. As a result, your emotional tie to the past clouds your good judgment. You still see yourself as a weak person who doesn't deserve any better and can't change your life.

The Family of Weakness

Think of your Desert of Weakness as a negative family of gossiping and critical relatives who are getting together for a family disunion. As they criticize and complain around the dinner table, you can easily recognize the weaknesses of the relatives by their mannerisms, vocal tone, and facial expressions.

At each part of the dinner table sits a haranguing relative who tries to make you feel bad and miserable. On one side of the table, you see "Papa Fear" espousing gloom and doom, "The world is coming to an end; your life is going to hell." On the other side of the table is "Mama Regret" who pounds you with all of the supposed mistakes you have committed in life, scolding you about, "All of the time you have wasted; look at how much you have ruined your life."

In the following chapters, you will sit at the table of disunion for a moment and meet the Weaknesses that torment you on a daily basis. You will learn techniques for defeating them, and you will kick them out of your life—once and for all.

Chapter Seven

The Rush Weakness

The Rush Weakness is the relentless inner voice that compels you to run, rush, and chase—to try to accomplish more than is realistically possible. It is the unforgiving taskmaster with a stopwatch, forever reminding you of how much you have to do, and how little time you have to do it in.

Try some self-analysis right now. Consider your daily schedule, and the many things you feel you must pack into it to "To get done what has to be done." In our technology-driven society, people expect quick answers and results. If you don't respond to someone quickly, they may be irritated or upset. They want you to rush to meet their timelines, no matter what. With the Rush Weakness pressuring you to move quickly, it seems that time becomes an enemy you cannot defeat.

The irony is that rushing often slows you down in the long run because you make mistakes that you later have to correct. When you speed and get into an accident, you are not going to get to your destination on time. If you cut corners and try to rush a relationship or financial situation, chances are it will go badly, and you will have to start over with a new person or investment.

How do you get away from the Rush Mentality? You need to develop The Mind of Patience.

Rush Antidote: The Mind of Patience

The Mind of Patience tells you that there is always enough time to do what needs to be done.

It is a mindset of relaxation, purpose, and focus. With the Mind of Patience, you take your time doing things right, which ends up saving you time in the long-run because you don't have to backtrack and fix your errors. Patience is so important to your Invincibility that we will cover it later in greater detail when we talk about Love Q: a higher form of psychological and spiritual intelligence.

As we discuss the Mind of Patience and the Rush Weakness, it's important that we make a distinction between acting quickly and decisively, and rushing.

Someone who rushes is caught up in an emotional tidal wave of fear, worry, and anxiety. Fear is what motivates them to rush. They are so concerned about not having enough time to do something that they often end up acting impulsively and making mistakes.

On the other hand, the quick-acting, decisive person knows exactly what they need to do. For example, an experienced first responder can react to a crisis with a relatively calm and proactive demeanor. They act quickly because they are not dominated by fear and anxiety. They know they have a job to do, and they can do it efficiently and quickly.

In the same way, the person who has the Mind of Patience recognizes the importance of deadlines and timeliness (a mother picks up her child from school at a certain time), while not being a slave to the emotional reactions of fear and worry about not having enough time. They are responsible, on time, and in control because the Rush Weakness doesn't dominate their mind.

Here's a way to increase your Mind of Patience when you are tempted to be impatient and rush around in a worried state:

Exercise: Choose the Longer Line

Many people hate to wait; for example, standing in a long line at a store. Yet, in reality, it's not the amount of time you have to wait that is the problem—it's the way your Rush-dominated mind adds a sense of impatience and discomfort to the waiting situation. Although waiting by itself can be a neutral experience, the Rush Weakness will make you dislike every minute of it.

To counteract your tendency toward impatience and the urge to rush, practice this exercise:

Intentionally choose the longer line at a store or any place where you have to wait. For example, you may be at a store or market, and you see a shorter line and a longer line. Most people will be inclined to dart to the shorter line so they can finish quicker and go home sooner.

You will do the opposite and stay in the longer line. When you do this, the Rush Weakness will attack you and say, "You're being foolish. Why are you slowing down your progress? Let's get out of here."

When you choose the longer line, you are telling the Rush Weakness to "Shut up." Despite its incessant jabbering, you are deciding to exercise your Patience Muscles. Think of patience as a muscle you can work on to make stronger. When you intentionally choose to stand in the longer line, you are increasing your capacity to wait peacefully, and in a relaxed manner, regardless of how impatient people are around you..

Plus, there are other benefits of waiting in line. You can observe your environment and fine-tune the skill of awareness: You can be aware of your thoughts and feelings and perhaps gain some insight about life and patience as you stand there. You can see how miserable other people are when they suffer under the dominion of the Rush Weakness—standing there impatiently, wringing their hands, shifting nervously, and complaining about how slow the line is, and how many important things they have to do. When you see how much they suffer from their rush mentality, you can decide to be different and enjoy a more relaxed pace of life.

Defeating the Rush Weakness with
The Mind of Patience

Many people in society are in a rush to obtain wealth, material prizes, love, success, approval, and contentment. Yet, by rushing with a Mind of Impatience, they often push themselves further away from their goals.

Impatience weakens their resolve, tempts them into making mistakes, and brings frustration and futility into their minds—making them chastise themselves because they aren't making more progress in their lives.

Although it may sound counterintuitive, keep in mind that the faster way (rushing) is often the slower way, and the slower way (patience) is usually the faster way. When you rush, you slow yourself down because you often have to go back to correct the mistakes you made by rushing. With the Mind of Patience, however, you actually obtain faster results because your mind is not distracted by the fear of failure—of not accomplishing everything you need to do in the limited time you have. With fewer distractions and less emotional turmoil, your mind is more focused and precise; consequently, you make fewer mistakes and you achieve better and faster results.

With the Mind of Patience, instead of fear, you have faith—that everything will turn out well. With faith, you learn how to wait even when you face the most seemingly difficult and frustrating situations—when people and circumstances appear to be against you; when you have failures and setbacks; when nothing goes your way. You will wait because you know that God (nature/reality) will bring you everything you need in due time; all you have to do is wait for the right people and situations to come into your life.

By activating your Mind of Patience, you will have more energy and motivation to persist at your goals. If at first you don't receive what you want—relationship, career, or financial success—you will keep working toward your goal with a Mind of Patience.

When you are tempted to rush and get things done faster, you will remind yourself of the saying: "The longer the wait, the better the prize." You know there is always something better in store for you if you keep working toward your desires. Never again will you allow the Rush Weakness to force you into an unwinnable race. Patience has become your sword, and you will rush no more.

Chapter Eight

....

The Anger Weakness

The Anger Weakness is the fiery thought that makes you explode with anger when you think that others are disrespecting you, or that life is unfair. This Anger Weakness is usually the result of a feeling of frustration or deprivation turned outward.

You are angry that you are not getting the money you deserve.

You are angry that people don't treat you the way you should be treated.

You are angry because your life doesn't turn out the way you want it to.

We live in a touchy world in which people are ready to come to verbal, and even physical blows, at the slightest perceived provocation. In certain large cities with congested highways, drivers have been known to explode into road rage—getting into fights and even pulling out weapons—because they believed the other driver was being disrespectful to them. Unfortunately, the end result is ultimately violence and human suffering.

If the Anger Weakness is such a pervasive part of our lives, what should we do to reduce its intensity and destructive tendencies? One of the best ways to master the Anger Weakness is to practice Anger Dissociation: Observe your anger without identifying with it—without thinking that it is you. Try this exercise:

Exercise: Anger Dissociation

The next time you're angry, be fully aware of yourself. Consciously feel the knot in your stomach, the burning sensation in your face, the desire to yell or attack someone (verbally or physically). Yet, you won't do anything about it. You won't release the anger, verbally or physically.

Instead, you will simply observe and dissociate yourself from the Anger Weakness. You will separate your true self, your Invincible Mind, from the hot burning coals of Anger.

Instead of labeling the sensation as "Anger," see it as a color, perhaps red. Visualize how this "Red" entity is howling and screaming, spoiling for a fight. You can sense its raw power and rage.

Yet, you also realize that *it is not you*. It is only something that is entering your mind momentarily. It is an uninvited guest. You can tell it to leave any time you want to.

Now visualize that this red entity is becoming smaller and smaller and is turning into a neutral color, perhaps white. As you watch the red entity diminish and turn white, you see that it becomes a little ball of white.

Finally, take a deep breath and visualize blowing it away as you say firmly, "I didn't invite you, Anger Weakness, and I don't want you in my life anymore. You can go now. Goodbye."

Anger versus Anger Weakness

As we examine the Anger Weakness, it's also important to recognize that the emotion of anger is different from the Anger Weakness.

There may be times when you need the emotion of anger. When you face danger, for example, anger can release certain brain chemicals that give you the strength and energy to fight back. When there is an injustice, or a horrible crime is committed against humanity, you can use some of anger's fiery force to make a statement or right a wrong.

The Anger Weakness, on the other hand, is an exaggerated form of ego slight that tries to tell you that "You are right," and "Everyone else is wrong for mistreating and disrespecting you." The Anger Weakness keeps you weak and controlled by its fiery nature—insisting that life or other people are unfair to you—demanding that you need to get what you deserve.

Fortunately, you can diminish the destructive force of the Anger Weakness by transmuting its fiery force into a sense of harmony and balance. Here's an exercise that can help you do that:

Anger Exercise: The Hands of Harmony

In the soft martial arts of Tai Chi and Aikido, you learn how to harmonize with your opponent, so that aggression can be turned into peace and cooperation. To help you reduce the Anger Weakness, here's a harmony exercise you can practice with a partner:

Step One: Face each other in a sideways stance with your legs spread apart about shoulder length, and with your forward leg slightly bent. Both you and your partner will bring your right hands together until they are touching at a point halfway between both of you. Both of your palms will be open and facing left.

Step Two: Now, slowly push back against your partner's hand as your partner slowly retracts their hand. Say to them: "This is my position; what I believe in."

Your partner will respond by saying: "I understand your point of view," as they slowly yield to your forward pressure while still maintaining a force that approximates, but is a bit less, than the force you are applying. Your partner will continue to allow their hand to be pushed back until it almost hits their chest.

Step Three: Now switch. Your partner will push your hand back as you allow it to retreat. Continue taking turns as each of you pushes, and is pushed, while taking turns repeating the phrases above—all the while being aware of your breathing as well as your emotional state.

During this exercise, you will discover that your breathing is slowing down, and that you are developing a peaceful and relaxed state of mind. Best of all, you will notice that you are creating a harmonious flow of motion with your partner that is matched by your verbal harmonizing with them—you and your partner are able to pick up on each other's energy level. Each of you senses the exact point at which the other begins to switch from a passive to an assertive mode of contact.

Try doing this exercise with your eyes closed. It will help you develop the feeling of Flow—that special sensation that occurs when you are in total harmony with another human being without having to prove that you are more powerful or aggressive than they are.

When this happens, you have temporarily merged your identity with the other person, while still retaining your own unique sense of self. You and the other person will take turns leading and following; extending and withdrawing, giving and taking—in a beautiful dance of blended energies and empathetic understanding.

Transform Anger into Harmony

As you begin to bring a sense of flow and harmony into your human interactions, you will be pleased at how relaxed and effective you are in dealing with other people. Instead of fighting against, and becoming angry with someone else's ideas or demands, you will have a sense of peace and acceptance. You will simply flow with whatever they are telling you.

When you do this, you are not being inauthentic or dishonest. Just like you did in the Hands of Harmony exercise, you are simply acknowledging their position, and then advancing your own, in a firm but peaceful way.

Although the Anger Weakness can be a stubborn foe, you can diminish its intensity and regain your calmness and composure. The key to defeating the Anger Weakness is non-reaction. Instead of reacting to the burning sensation inside you—saying or doing something you will later regret—you will focus on feeling the fiery sensations with full awareness; without fearing them or letting them control you. You will say to yourself, "There is a temporary burning sensation inside me; I feel it fully and it will pass from me. It is not me: It is simply a temporary storm that will quickly disappear from my life. I am in charge."

In the beginning, it may be difficult for you to control the Anger Weakness; it has a tendency to take you over—it may even feel good at times to explode with rage and anger (although later you feel the pain and regret). Yet, the more you practice experiencing anger fully without reacting to it—seeing it as a color or outside entity that temporarily invades you—the quicker you will recover from its attack on your self-control.

With practice, you will be able to control the Anger Weakness; you will only keep its positive elements (anger that motivates for positive change) while keeping out its destructive parts. Now, instead of the Anger Weakness, you have harmony and peace. You no longer feel that you are hitting yourself against the wall of frustration and denial of what you want. You simply flow and harmonize with whatever life and other people bring you, and you feel joyous and content every step of the way.

Chapter Nine

The Regret Weakness

There is a weakness that ties you to the past and makes you suffer for every real or imagined mistake that you have ever made. It is called the Regret Weakness: the insidious thought that you have screwed up your life and made a mess of it because of your past mistakes.

The Regret Weakness is relentless in telling you that you can never repair the damage you have done; that you will always feel like a loser because of the errors and blunders you have made, and will continue to make. The trickiest thing about the Regret Weakness is that when you feel bad about your choices, you tend to repeat the same mistakes because you don't feel worthy or smart enough to do any better.

Your emotional tie to the past is what ends up destroying your feelings of self-worth. The Regret Weakness will make you see yourself as weak or a loser in a specific area; for example, in relationships or business matters. Regardless of your perceived area of weakness, the Regret Weakness will home in on your self-attacking thought that "You should have done better."

Of course, everyone makes mistakes; our judgment is sometimes clouded; our willpower may be weak. The problem is not the mistake per se, but your reactions to the mistake—self-attacks engineered by the Self-Defeating Mind which tell you that you are inferior, foolish, or inadequate because of your mistakes.

The solution is to realize that self-accusation has no place in your present day because you are becoming a different person. Guided by your Invincible Mind, you can learn from your mistakes and improve on your past—facing the future with optimism and hope.

The Magic of Staying the Same in Time

Once, there was an unhappy middle-aged woman who visited a magician. She was stuck in an unhappy marriage for many years and had never fulfilled her dream to be a concert violinist. Instead, she had worked in corporate law and hated every minute of it, even though she had been well-compensated.

The magician hypnotized her and took her back in time to relive her past and attempt to change it. As she went back in time, she found herself falling in love again with the handsome and charismatic man who would later turn out to be her cold and emotionally abusive husband. She couldn't resist marrying him at the time because she was mesmerized by the chemistry they had together.

When her husband suggested that she become a corporate lawyer like her father, she visualized having a luxurious lifestyle for their family, and she began to crave it. She found herself giving up her dream career of being a concert violinist and taking up the highly lucrative, but unsatisfying career (for her), of corporate law.

As the magician brought her back to the present, tears filled her eyes, and she realized the truth:

"I could not have acted any differently because what I thought was important at the time is what I got. Before, I valued the superficial—surface looks and charisma; glamour and material extravagance—instead of what I really wanted, which was to be a creative artist and have a loving family."

The clever and compassionate magician smiled and told her the truth:

"Yes, there is nothing to regret. There is nothing you could have changed because the person you were at the time would have made the same choices, even if given 100 lifetimes. The good news is that you no longer have to be that person. Starting today, you can choose your True Self and live a new life without fear, and without regrets.

How to Defeat Regret: Allow Yourself to Go Back

Many times, people take an "All or Nothing" perfectionistic approach to their weakness or bad habits. They think, "Either I completely change my old negative habits today, or I'm a total failure."

The better approach is to "Allow Yourself to Go Back"—give yourself a break if you fall back into an old temptation, bad habit, or negative behavior. Instead of condemning yourself as a weak or unworthy person, practice self-compassion and tell yourself that you can get back on track and be a stronger person as a result of the temporary step back.

When you are too hard on yourself for returning to a negative behavior or destructive habit, you will tend to fall into an emotional place of weakness and regret. Consequently, you are likely to repeat the same self-defeating actions that made you feel weak in the first place because you don't believe you deserve any better.

The truth is that you probably didn't develop a weakness or bad habit overnight. It took you many steps to slide down into the Desert of Weakness to reach this stage. Consequently, since you fell down little by little, you need to gradually pull yourself out over time.

Recognize this simple truth: Weakness attracts more weakness.

For example, let's say that you are trying to quit drinking energy drinks that contain a lot of sugar—you know they are not healthy for you and make you gain weight. You make an oath to yourself that you're quitting. You're fine going several days without drinking one, but then on a hot, stressful day, you yield to temptation and have one.

Feeling bad about your choice to imbibe the energy drink, the Regret Weakness taunts you, "You blew your regimen. You have no discipline. You may as well drink another one." If you believe what the Regret Weakness is telling you (you lack self-discipline), you may be tempted to go back to drinking energy drinks. You're caught in a downward spiral of weakness.

Things are much different when you allow yourself to go back and forgive yourself for a previous error or lapse in judgment. You can move on from the momentary lack of willpower—drinking the beverage—and go back to your disciplined plan immediately. You know you can still make progress toward a healthier lifestyle.

Exercise: Recreate a Memory:
The Re-Imprinting Experience

One of the obstacles we face in achieving Invincibility is dealing with bad memories and regrets from our past that keep intruding into our consciousness—making us feel weak and defeated. What do we do with regretful memories of loss, failure, and trauma? There is a certain Re-Imprinting Experience you can use to reprogram your memories so they no longer haunt or control you.

Here's what you need to do:

Step One: Think of a situation that didn't work out the way you wanted it to. Relive what it looked like, sounded like, and felt like. What were your facial expressions like? What was your level of calmness or agitation? How about your tone of voice? How were you received by others?

Step Two: Center Yourself: Breathe deeply. Scan your body for points of tension and relax them. Visualize that the tension in your body is slowly melting like butter. Further imagine that you are standing upright and you are balanced, confident, and relaxed.

Step Three: Reexperience the Situation From a Higher Mental Place: Now go back mentally and imagine yourself in the past—except this time see yourself acting in the way you would act if you had the knowledge of today—as a wiser, more experienced, and stronger person. Hear yourself speaking in a sincere, peaceful, and confident tone. Observe the many unforeseen benefits that occur as you relive the scenario.

For example, think back to a very heated argument you had with a close friend, lover, or family member in which you said things that were harsh or difficult to say, and the relationship was severely and irreparably damaged. Although you may have been justified in what you said, perhaps you felt guilty, sad, or regretful because you lost an important person in your life.

Now, when you go back mentally, and reexperience the situation with a more mature and elevated mindset, you see things differently. You see the good that came from the blow up. Perhaps the person was toxic and bad for you. You take note of the lesson you learned: that you will stand up for yourself when facing negative and abusive people. You also decide that you will focus on developing positive relationships, while staying away from negative and damaging ones.

With this exercise, you have changed your past. Instead of feeling regret about the past conflict, you have imprinted a new thought in your mind, otherwise known as Loving Memory. Loving Memory is the wisdom that you gain from any experience, whether you call what happened to you good or bad. This wisdom ultimately helps you become a more loving person—toward yourself and others.

In the future, when you suffer pain, you will take the lesson from the pain and transform it into a valuable piece of wisdom (Loving Memory). This wisdom will, in turn, restructure your previous bad memory—leaving you with a positive mental feeling about the experience instead of the previous bitter and regretful one you had before.

Live A Regret-Free Life

When you forgive yourself for past mistakes, you recognize the lessons learned, and you avoid repeating the same actions. Your goal is to improve the way you react to your environment and life situations. As a result, you feel better about yourself in the process. You become stronger and more determined. You are better able to withstand the temptation to go back to your old self-defeating ways such as procrastination, bad habits, and poor relationship choices.

Always remember that being under the influence of your Self-Defeating Mind is like being hypnotized by an evil magician. The magician makes you do things that are harmful to you, but you can't seem to resist it. Once you break free of the spell, you are no longer hypnotized, and you no longer condemn yourself for your past. You realize that at the time you couldn't have acted any better because you were under the spell of a malevolent influence. Now that you have broken free, you awaken to your true self—your Invincible Mind—and you no longer hate yourself for something you did in the past.

When you are freed from your old hypnotized self, you break your connection with the past and the mistakes you made; you see yourself differently. You no longer label yourself as destructive, weak, or stupid. Instead, you recognize your Invincible Self.

From this day forward, be aware of when the Regret Weakness tries to push itself into your mind and tries to make you feel weak and inadequate because of past mistakes. If you catch the Regret Weakness trying to enter you, quickly switch your mindset from Regret ("If only, I had done this differently") to Hope ("Next time I will do better").

Don't waste mental energy brooding over past events, decisions, and actions—look forward instead of backwards. Always head toward "next time"—the best and most optimistic place to be.

Chapter Ten

....

The Futility Weakness

The Futility Weakness is an emotional killer. It is the thought that you are being deprived of the good things in life; that you are living beneath your potential; that you are doomed to be a failure. It may weigh you down with an overall feeling of failure and deprivation, or it may target a particular area in your life in which you feel unfulfilled—perhaps your finances, career, relationships, health, or happiness.

Although you may have your moments of pleasure, success, and contentment, the Futility Weakness doesn't let you enjoy them for very long—it keeps you feeling sad, depressed, and futile because it tells you that you have never lived up to your fullest potential. It tells you that you have squandered opportunities, and now it's too late to accomplish what you truly want.

The Futility Weakness may come from the voices of influential people from your past ("You keep screwing up"), or it could be a creation of your own mind which chastises you for failures and frustrations in your life—whether in love, work, finances, relationships, or personal habits.

Although the Futility Weakness may appear to be a strong influence in your life, there is good news: You can defeat the Futility Weakness by recognizing that it is only an imaginary echo in your mind that has nothing to do with the real Invincible You. Your true essence, your powerful Invincible nature, is far stronger than any momentary thoughts of failure or defeat.

Here are some Futility Erasing techniques that can help jolt you out of a futility mindset, and into a mind that is bursting with confidence and possibilities.

Futility Eraser Number One: Create an Attitude of Selective Attention

Here's a powerful technique for erasing the Futility Weakness:

Step One: During the next week, begin to focus on all of the good things that have happened in your life. To help you remember, walk around your house and find material objects that remind you of happy and successful times.

For example, in your bedroom, you may become aware of a special picture of a loved one or pet, a gift given to you by a close family member or special friend, a trophy or certificate (award) that represents a triumph you enjoyed.

Step Two: As you look at each item, say the word, "Yeah!" with enthusiasm. Each time you find something that reminds you of a good emotional moment, say "Yeah!" with greater intensity and volume.

If you can't find anything in your home that brings back positive memories, think of a time when you felt happy, successful, or loved. Vividly see yourself in that situation—recall the sights, sounds, and feelings of that moment. Maybe, you had a graduation, a success at work, or a loving moment with a special person or animal. As you recall these special happiness moments, say the word, "Yeah!" with increasing power and enthusiasm.

Step Three: As you build your level of excitement and well-being to its ultimate peak, add a physical dimension to the experience. Perform a physical activity—dance, run, clap your hands, or do jumping jacks.

Step Four: Feel the blood and adrenaline surge through your body as you say forcefully, and with confidence: "I am strong, powerful, loving, and Invincible. I can do anything I want. I am a success!"

This exercise, if practiced consistently, can help you diminish your Futility Mindset and move you into a state of Invincibility. You can master the Futility Weakness as long as you congruently express your new sense of confidence through every aspect of your identity—your physique, voice, and thought processes.

Futility Eraser Number Two: Step into the Circle of Power

Practice this exercise to diminish the Futility Weakness in your life:

Step One: At your home or office, imagine an invisible circle on the floor—three feet in diameter and two feet in front of you. You will call this the "Circle of Power."

Step Two: Recall a time when you were at your most successful and powerful—you were witty, bright, fun-loving, joyful, and loved by others. If you can't quite remember such a time, think of a scene from a movie in which your favorite movie hero or heroine is enjoying a powerful and joyous moment. Picture yourself as that person.

Step Three: Now step into the imaginary circle and stand there quietly. Firmly grasp your right shoulder with your left hand, give it a squeeze, and repeat the following phrase: "I am stepping into the circle of power. I share the power of the Universe. I am Invincible."

As you say the above phrase, you will find yourself feeling more powerful and competent. By linking previous feelings of success with the circle, and the squeeze on your shoulder, you are developing a "cue association."

A cue association is a psychological tool that allows you to link certain powerful feelings with a particular physical act or gesture. In this case, the touch on the shoulder, as well as stepping into an imaginary circle, will trigger in you feelings and thoughts of joy, competence, and self-confidence.

In the future, whenever you need a psychological boost in your battle against the Futility Weakness, you can step into the imaginary circle of power as you grasp your right shoulder with your left hand. When you do this, you will be pleasantly surprised at how quickly you can change your state of mind from one that is dominated by the Futility Weakness to one that is carefree and roaring with confidence.

True Confidence Can Be Yours

Futility is often the end result of many other weaknesses. It is the desire to give up; to blame others, and life itself, for all the bad that has happened to you. It is the frustration of hitting your head against the wall, of not being able to achieve your goals—in your relationships, finances, career, health, and happiness.

Although Futility appears to be a solid barrier in front of your success and happiness, realize this: Futility is not reality. It is nothing more than a fictitious and short-lived perception of failure that has no real hold over you. It's power to influence you will vanish once you decide that you, and no one else, is ultimately responsible for your own happiness.

Think of a prison cell in which the bars are made of soft tissue paper—yet are painted to look like solid metal bars. At first glance, you see no way out—no way to escape. But, then you receive a letter from a prisoner who escaped and told you the truth: The bars are really nothing but paper—you can easily break through them and escape to freedom.

In the same way, realize that the Futility Weakness is nothing more than falsely painted mental bars. You can easily burst through them to psychological freedom once you realize what they really are.

By conscientiously applying the strategies in this chapter, you can begin to transform yourself from a person who is under the dominion of futility into an energetic person full of energy, confidence, and faith.

As you begin to live a truly confident life, you will stop dwelling on your supposedly hopeless and futile state, and you will start to realize how much power of choice you really have. In the end, you will happily discover that there is no such thing as futility or defeat because everything can be used to improve the most important thing in your life: Your Invincible nature.

Chapter Eleven

The Fear Weakness

The Fear Weakness is the foundation for a lot of your other negativities. It keeps you in fear of losing out in life and suffering from disappointment, failure, rejection, and pain. It makes you fear unexpected financial expenses, failing in your career or relationships, being unnoticed or unloved, and being cheated or deprived.

The Fear Weakness is actually a part of many negative emotions: Loneliness is the fear of being alone; depression is the fear of losing, or having lost, something important to you. Fear also manifests itself as tension and worry.

One thing to recognize, however, is that the emotion of fear is different from the Fear Weakness.

Fear is an emotion that can have beneficial functions. It can warn you of danger and give you the chemical boost you need to fight or run. It can protect you from doing hazardous things like touching a hot stove.

The Fear Weakness, on the other hand, is an exaggerated and often unrealistic fear about bad things that may never happen.

Many people in society have a deeply rooted anxiety. They worry, "What will happen to me tomorrow?" They strain over future finances, relationships, and health. They hope their lives will improve, or at least not worsen, but their hope is fearful—they sense their lack of control over the future.

If you think about it, you will realize that The Fear Weakness is nothing more than an artificial accumulation of all the unrealistic and irrational fears you have ever experienced in your life. These include fears such as "I'm going to lose out," "I'm not going to get what I want," and "Life (or people) will hurt me."

The Fear Weakness' sole job is to torment you about things that usually have a small chance of occurring in reality.

The Fear Weakness Comes in Several Varieties

Here are some common Fear Weaknesses. Fear of:

- Displeasing others

- Being helpless in the future

- A weakness you can't control such as addictions, bad habits, and unproductive behaviors

- Absence of excitement, also known as boredom

- Exposure of fakery: People finding out that you are not as good as they thought you were

- Financial expenses that can't be handled

- Sickness, old age, and death

- Being unnoticed, unwanted, rejected, and unloved

- Being cheated and left out of things

- Being alone and lonely—never finding anyone to love

- Inability to change yourself

The list of Fear Weaknesses goes on and on.

Although the Fear Weakness comes in different varieties, most of them stem from the same root: They are based on attachments to fixed mental and emotional positions such as, "You must be loved by a particular person," "You must make x amount of money," and "You must be liked and appreciated by x type of people."

By insisting that you must have something, you create the opposite possibility that you will not get what you want. This keeps you feeling nervous, tense, and fearful because you identify with whatever it is you want—you build your self-esteem based on obtaining the prize or benefit. Then, when you don't get what you want, or if you lose it, you may feel that you have lost an important piece of yourself—resulting in frustration, disappointment, and sadness.

The Fear of Money Loss

One of the biggest fears people have is that they will lose money, or not have enough of it. This fear is found in the poor as well as the rich.

For example, a person may love money to the exclusion of everything else. If you try to separate them from their money, they will become fearfully hostile. They may think: "What would I be like without my money?" If you tell them that their excessive emotional attachment to money actually makes them poor, they will respond with thinly veiled anger, or a polite smile that hides a disagreeable and hostile opinion.

Although money, used rightly, can be a great gift, everything depends on the mindset of the person holding the money. A person (rich or poor) with an enlightened mindset can enjoy their money because they recognize that their inner worth does not depend on their outer net worth. They recognize that true wealth comes from their Invincible Mind.

On the other hand, a person with a selfish and cheap mentality toward money is dominated by fear—the fear that they will lose their money, and in the process, lose their self-worth. There are tightwads among both the rich and the poor. What they have in common is that they emotionally attach their value as a human being to how much money they have. Therefore, they base their ego on a shaky foundation that keeps them feeling nervous and fearful of losing what they already have.

Fear and the Miser

There once was a very cheap man who only brought a quarter with him to leave a tip at the diner he frequented. When he went out with friends, he conveniently "forgot" his wallet so his friends would have to pay the bill. Pretty soon, he didn't have any friends because they knew how much of a tightwad he was, and they resented the way he tried to take advantage of them.

One day, the tightwad man lost all of his money in a bad investment and ended up homeless—he had no family or friends who would take him in. Months passed, and he roamed the city with his little bag of belongings. Each day, he grew more disheveled, lonely, and bitter.

Eventually, he settled into a spot close to the diner where he used to go all the time. Sitting with his few belongings on the sidewalk, he would see one of the waitresses who used to serve him, and he recalled how he used to give her a 25 cent tip. Every morning, the waitress would quietly come out and bring him fresh orange juice and a bagel with cream cheese, paid from her own pocket.

Sometimes, she brought him deli meats and fruit, as well. She never said anything, but just brought it to him, with a smile and a "Hello."

Too embarrassed to make eye contact, Mr. Miser would take the food and drink and mumble a quick "Thank you."

Finally, Mr. Miser got up the courage and asked her, "Do you recognize me?"

"Yes," she nodded. "You are the gentleman who used to come in here and give us a 25 cent tip."

"I know; I was very cheap to you. Why are you helping me now?"

She replied with a heartfelt smile: "Because you are a human being worthy of help. I am not financially rich—I barely make ends meet. But, I am grateful that I can give to those who need it. And, you need it."

"I'm sorry, I don't know what to say."

"You don't have to say anything. Helping you is all the thanks I need. I give and I receive from the goodness of giving. It's as simple as that."

Tears filled the Miser's eyes. He knew he had lost more than money in his life—he had lost his goodwill toward humanity. And, this small example of goodness gave him hope. Maybe he didn't have to be a miser after all.

Master the Fear Weakness

To master the Fear Weakness, and its toxic family members—anxiety, worry, and doubt—you need to work daily to maintain awareness of when unreasonable thoughts of fear try to invade your mind. Then, you need to take the right steps to make sure that the Fear Weakness doesn't maintain permanent residence in your mind.

Here's the good news: if you learn how to master the Fear Weakness, you can immediately defeat many other weaknesses and solve a myriad of problems. When you start to eradicate the Fear Weakness, you realize how you worry less about bills; you stress less about time pressures; you are less self-conscious about looking foolish in social situations; you are less fearful about taking intelligent risks at work or with your finances. Once one Fear Weakness domino starts to fall, the rest will fall as you begin to live more confidently, joyfully, and purposefully.

Let's begin your Fear Weakness Eradication Journey. Here are some ways to diminish unreasonable fear in your life:

Method #1: Create a Fear to Reality Journal

Try this exercise: During your day, observe how many times your mind slips into the fear of what tomorrow may bring. When you recognize the Fear Weakness, bring yourself to the present moment. Take a deep breath, look around, and scan your surroundings. Realize that the Fear Weakness only exists in your imagination. Nothing bad has happened to you yet; you are still living in the present. You are OK right now.

To bring more objectivity into your fears, create a Fear to Reality Journal. Write down all of the things you are afraid of, and then check periodically to see if they have come true.

You will find that a majority of your fears related to money, love, health, possessions, or career/business don't come true in the way you feared. You will see that fear can consume your present and prevent you from fully enjoying life. And for what? Most of what you worried about never came true in the way you envisioned it. This realization will help liberate you from many of the fears that torment you on a daily basis.

By keeping a journal and reality testing your fears like this, you will take the first step toward mastering the Fear Weakness. Soon, you will get to the point where your worrying self no longer exists, or if it does, it is very faint and ineffectual.

Method #2: Ask the Right Questions

Another way to master the Fear Weakness is to ask yourself the right questions.

For example, ask yourself: "What would I do if I had nothing to fear?"

When you ask yourself this question, you immediately reverse the paradigm—from fear to belief. You start to think of the things you *can* do (belief) instead of what you *can't* do (fear). You immediately focus on the new relationships, career choices, and lifestyle changes you would like to achieve. You have more energy and motivation to accomplish your goals and desires.

Another good question to ask is, "Who is living your life?"

If the Desert of Weakness is living your life for you, you will continue to suffer from the Fear Weakness. On the other hand, if the Mountain of Invincibility is representing your mind, you will realize that you are not your Fear Weakness—you are something much higher and more powerful. You are a person with personal power who can conquer your problems despite fear and negativity.

Method #3: Take Action Despite the Thought

Still another valuable tool in your anti-Fear Weakness arsenal is the technique known as Action Despite the Thought:

You will take action while still having the fear thoughts inside your mind.

When you feel overwhelmed and paralyzed with fear ("I will look foolish"; "I will be rejected"; "I will fail"), decide that you will do what you need to do, despite your anxiety. You will talk to that attractive person, go for the career you want, make the financial investment you've been thinking about, start that creative project you love.

This is a very powerful principle because when you act despite the fear, you reverse the game on the Fear Weakness. You paralyze it with your boldness. You take steps toward your goals despite the specter of fear hovering over you. When you do this, you call the bluff on the Fear Weakness, and you see that, like all bullies, it will retreat once you stand up to it.

Many times, we are reluctant to make a change in our lives because of fear. We say that we want to "wait until the right moment," "until conditions are right," or "until I have inspiration to do it."

Here's a little secret: If you wait until conditions are perfectly right, you will never do what you want to do. Fear will always tell you that it's not the right time.

A good example is a writer who waits for inspiration to strike before they write. One of the worst fears of a writer is known as "writer's block"—when a writer feels anxiety about writing because they don't think their writing will be good enough. As a result, they feel blocked from writing; no matter how hard they try, they can't manufacture words on the page.

Sometimes, blocked writers receive advice such as "Wait until the inspiration moves you." That is false advice because if you wait for the inspiration to move you, you may never write anything because you are waiting until something happens, instead of making something happen.

The better advice is "Rather than wait for inspiration to move you, *you move the inspiration.*"

Sit down and work (write, for example) to move the inspiration in your favor. The more you work, and the more action you take, the more inspiration will be on your side. When you take action despite the fear, you bypass the fear of failure or rejection. You move beyond the fear into the achievement of your goal.

Start now. Think of the things you want in life, but are afraid to go for, because you fear rejection or failure. Also, think of actions you can take toward their attainment:

If you want to buy a house, speak to an agent and study some listings.

If you want to get a good education, research schools and requirements.

If you want to fall in love, look into dating options such as online dating and social networking.

If you want to get your body in shape, join a gym and spend at least 20 minutes there daily, as you build up your workout tolerance.

If you want to write the Great American Novel, sit down and write three pages of "junk" daily—whatever comes to your mind. It may actually be quite good, but you will tell yourself that you will write down whatever comes to your mind—whether it is good or bad. By doing this, you take the paralyzing pressure off yourself to be perfect, and you can relax and let your creativity flow.

Whatever your dream is, decide today to take concrete and practical steps toward it. You will take action despite the thought; despite the fear of failure or rejection.

By utilizing action despite the thought (of fear), you will be amazed at how much progress you can make in your inner and outer life. Combining this technique with the Fear to Reality Journal and Asking the Right Questions, you will begin to eliminate the Fear Weakness from your mind. As a result, you will find that your motivation is strong, and your results are undeniable.

Have Dinner with Your Invincible Mind Family

Now that you have learned techniques for defeating your Weaknesses, you have a clear path to transform your Desert of Weakness into a Mountain of Invincibility—a holding place for all of your positive thoughts and emotions: joy, courage, resilience, compassion, love, and goodwill.

The good news is that you have a positive and healthy side of your mental family: The Invincible Mind Family. When they get together, there is "Papa Joy" on one side of the table, and sitting next to him is "Mama Compassion." These light and healing forces in your life are powerful, good, and benevolent. These are the positive and healing thought guides that you can draw from to reach true happiness.

Whenever you feel like you are falling into the grips of your Self-Defeating nature, focus on Invincibility Thought words to rejuvenate yourself. These are words such as "naturalness," "spontaneity," "receptivity," "self-renewal," "insight," "persistence," "self-unity," "patience," "compassion," and "love." These are the beautiful words that will liberate you from the Desert of Weakness.

How do you distinguish between Invincible Thoughts and Self-Defeating Thoughts? Listen to what the thoughts tell you. If they are positive and healing, they are Invincible Thoughts. If they are negative and self-attacking, they are Self-Defeating thoughts. Imagine a dialogue between the two as they compete to win over the space in your mind.

The Self-Defeating Thoughts say things like: "I want to keep you desperate, afraid, sad, and disillusioned. If it were up to me, you would feel defeated all of the time. I want you to suffer."

The Invincible Thoughts say, "I want you to prosper, grow, love, succeed, and help humanity. My desire is that you become the best person you can possibly be, and that you live with love and true inner power."

Another way to look at this is to say that Self-Defeating Thoughts want what is worse for you, while Invincible Thoughts want what is best for you. When you start to enhance your Invincible Thoughts, you will also realize that you have to put forth some effort. Invincible Thoughts will not start the walk for you, but they will match every step you take with a step of their own toward you.

The good news is that one Invincible Thought—for example, peace—can wipe away a dozen Self-Defeating Thoughts such as fear, anger, and regret. As you wake up from the hypnotic spell forced on you by the Self-Defeating Mind, you will see that your compulsive cravings—the nervous need for approval, excessive acquisition, and overstated ego—are part of your Self-Defeating Mind. As these false desires vanish, you will become a more loving and balanced human being. When this happens, you will chuckle in amusement at the childish attempts of fear and worry to bring you down. You have no more time to fool around with the things that used to bother you; they have no power to disturb the real you.

Before long, you will distance yourself from the Desert of Weakness. You will live from an elevated state of mind, the Mountain of Invincibility: a place that is peaceful, confident, powerful, loving, and pure. You will have everything you need.

Chapter Twelve

....

Your Mountain of Invincibility

Your Mountain of Invincibility is the part of your mind that holds positive thoughts and emotions—patience, peace, love, and confidence—and helps you overcome obstacles so you can prosper in life.

Like a mountain in the physical world, this is the part of your mind that is clean, pure, and elevated. Instead of being clouded by negativity and self-doubt, your thoughts are more realistic, precise, and optimistic. From your Mountain of Invincibility, you have a completely new perspective on the problems that used to bother you; the worries that used to paralyze you. Because you are at an elevated mental place, you realize that your potential for greatness is much stronger than your fears, self-doubts, and feelings of inadequacy; at the peak of your Invincibility, you feel peaceful, compassionate, triumphant.

In everyday life, your Mountain of Invincibility is your ultimate source of creativity, talent, motivation, energy, and resilience. When problems and frustrations mount, and nothing you do seems to work, your Mountain of Invincibility is what gives you great power to live the way you truly desire.

How do you reach the heights of your Mountain of Invincibility? There are a few simple things you can do to access the energy and brilliance of this stronghold of inner strength.

Develop Relentless Confidence: The Winning Trait

A good way to tap into your Mountain of Invincibility is to develop the success trait known as Relentless Confidence: the heightened state of self-belief that leads you to excellence. It is relentless in the sense that you never give up the belief that you will excel and prosper in life. You know you will triumph and prosper, and that is exactly what will happen.

Relentless Confidence occurs when you shift your thoughts toward the things—people, circumstances, and higher power—that are *for* you, instead of the things that are *against* you.

With Relentless Confidence, you focus on the vast power that is on your side. You think constantly of your higher God (nature)-given abilities, instead of your difficulties. You don't allow problems to grow into enormous sizes that can defeat you—you become bigger than your obstacles.

Recognize, however, that Relentless Confidence is not puffed-up ego, arrogance, or selfishness.

On the contrary, it is a realistic and humble appreciation of who you are as a human being—someone who has been gifted with wonderful talents such as creativity, nurturing, teaching, or hands-on abilities. You are a unique human being who has been put on Earth to use those talents for the good of yourself and others.

With Relentless Confidence, you calmly accept a problem or obstacle as part of the pattern of life. You know you can turn it into your advantage. You think, "I rejoice when I have problems because I am superior to them. I will think my way around them, over them, or through them. Each problem has a solution and solving the problem makes me stronger."

When you're able to get beyond your problems and recover from failures, you have a sense of excitement. You have a realization that you have what it takes to handle anything and everything that comes your way.

When life throws a dagger at you, there are two ways you can catch it: By the blade or by the handle. If you catch it by the blade—taking it with a negative, "pity me" mindset—it can cut and injure you. If you catch it by the handle, with confidence and hope, you can use it to fight your way through any obstacle.

Bill, a sales manager in his early-60s, had always been a confident and proud man. Working his way up the corporate ladder, he had excelled in his work and was well-liked by subordinates and supervisors alike. Then he got the news: He was being laid off due to a budget cut. He couldn't believe this was happening to him. He had intended to work at least ten more years before retirement—he loved his work and was good at it.

Depression hit him—what would he do now? He and his wife were OK financially, but he asked himself, "What will I do with my time?" "How will my life be meaningful?" After several months of inactivity since being let go, he hit on the answer: He and his wife would start a nonprofit charity for rescuing animals. They had four dogs ranging from a Chihuahua to a Pit Bull, and they loved animals. Working closely together, Bill and his wife started their nonprofit charity.

In the process, they renewed their love for each other and received great satisfaction every time they placed lost animals in a loving home.

Currently, Bill is using his sales skills to raise funds and public awareness for animal rights. He is having a great time. He is even thankful that being laid off offered him an opportunity to contribute to society and enjoy himself at the same time. He says he isn't in the retirement stage; he is in the "refinement stage," refining what he wants to do with the rest of his life. He's looking forward to it.

Be a How Thinker

Decide today to act differently when faced with a big obstacle. Instead of cowering from it, let a challenge arouse your fighting spirit. With the Relentless Confidence Mindset, you become a "How" versus an "If" thinker.

"How" thinkers talk about how they can stage a comeback. When they experience a momentary setback, they think: "How can I get back on track?" If they see that their happiness is being limited, they find the block—the bad habit or self-defeating mindset—and they remove it.

"If" thinkers, on the other hand, lament everything they have ever done. They feel defeated and have a sense of futility about achieving their dreams. Feeling sorry for themselves, they say, "If only I had done this better." As a result, the next time they try something, they already feel defeated. They end up giving up too early, or they don't try very hard, because they fear repeating the same mistakes (They often do).

When you become a How Thinker, you will enjoy plenty of victories. You will have little competition because most people are "If" thinkers. As a How Thinker, you are part of an elite group of individuals who never give up until they accomplish their goals.

A marvelous example of a How thinker is the story of David Goggins, a former U.S. Navy SEAL who completed a 100-mile ultramarathon despite kidney damage and broken bones. Suffering from severe pain during the race, Goggins kept telling himself that he was the toughest, strongest, and most determined person on Earth. He believed it, and he finished the race—a perfect example of a How Thinker.

With a positive and relentless success-seeking mindset, you can become a How Thinker. As a result, you will conquer your inner world of thoughts and feelings, as well as the outer world of people and circumstances.

Pay the Price for Upward Mental Mobility

There is one thing you need to know as you begin to release the power of your Mountain of Invincibility: To be Invincible, you must first pay the price. The price you pay for the higher states of existence like well-being and love is to give up the lower states such as anger, regret, and anxiety. In reality, you are not giving up anything of true value;

you are simply trading junk (Self-Defeating thoughts) for something valuable (Invincible Thoughts). Here's how you do it:

Think of a lower state you want to give up; for example, anger. Perhaps, you become irritated too easily when you're driving and people ahead of you are going too slowly. You may be tempted to yell at them to hurry up, or you may even use some curse words to get back at them. At the moment that you yell and lose your temper, you may feel a surge of temporary excitement or empowerment. Yet, later you may feel bad that you lost your cool and created a scene.

Your next step is to decide what state you would like to replace the anger with; in this case, with peace. Each time you're driving, and there is a slow driver ahead of you, you will become aware of your anger boiling up, and you will intentionally choose the state of peace. You will say to yourself, "I choose peace over anger at this moment. I exchange the fiery feelings of anger, the burning sensations of hostility, for a calm and serene sense of peace."

When you do this, your mindset will start to change; you will become more patient and tolerant. Best of all, you will be healthier and happier because you have exchanged a negative state such as anger for a positive state like peace.

Now think of other states you can give up to gain something much better.

If you want a healthy body, you need to give up emotional eating— eating when you're sad or upset.

If you want relaxation, you need to give up rushing.

If you want financial security, you need to give up the fear of making a wrong financial investment.

If you want true romantic love, you must give up false substitutes such as superficial sex or casual relationships.

Each time you sacrifice the lower for the higher, you take one step closer toward attaining your goals: great relationships, career and economic success, personal mastery, and happiness.

Here's an important truth: To receive true psychological treasure such as contentment and peace, you need to first take out the mental trash. Every time you get rid of a bad habit—getting angry quickly, eating when you're sad—you receive payment in the form of higher emotional states such as peace and self-confidence.

You realize the truth: The faster you pay for emotional treasure by giving up mental trash, the quicker you will receive permanent riches, also known as mental treasure.

The Unusual Storekeeper

There once was a storekeeper who had an unusual business. In the front of his store, a sign read: "Trades Accepted. Exchange Anger for Compassion, Rushing for Relaxation, Selfishness for Love, and Sadness for Happiness."

One curious passerby went in and asked the storekeeper, "This is an amazing business you are running. You must get a lot of customers."

"Not really," replied the storekeeper sadly. "Some people don't value my products. Some don't believe that items like compassion actually exist. Others come in to angrily and righteously tell me that they already have love, peace, and happiness—they don't need my services. Others try to sell me their gloom and doom, but I politely decline.

How about you? Would you be interested in a real trade that can change your life?"

"I'm sorry, but I've got to get back to work. I'm already late and pressed for time."

"OK, I'm always here if you need me," said the storekeeper with a compassionate smile as the potential customer rushed out of the store.

Although he didn't make a lot of sales, the storekeeper knew that the best customers were aware individuals who had suffered in life carrying around their mental junk disguised as treasure. Once they had enough pain and despair, they were finally ready to exchange their trash for items of real value: compassion, peace, and goodwill.

It's unfortunate that many people don't realize just how important it is for them to trade their negative and worthless mental states, such as excessive and unrealistic fear and anger, for true psychological prizes like peace, confidence, and love.

How about you? All you have to do is make the trade and give up what you don't really need for the thoughts and feelings that will bring you lasting joy and well-being. Although turning pain into power sounds like an inherently practical and useful concept, many people are afraid to do it. They are afraid because they think they will lose something valuable if they give up their old ways—their false excitement, useless involvements, and self-defeating activities.

They *will* lose something: the mental trash that has been filling up the mansion of their mind. They will lose their Self-Defeating thoughts—their obsessive thoughts patterns, downcast feelings, and compulsive behaviors.

Exercise: Dump Your Mental Junk

Here's a useful exercise to help you get rid of adverse thoughts and feelings:

Make a list of all the mental junk you want to get rid of. Write down your Self-Defeating thoughts on a piece of paper. You may write down things such as:

- The thought that you're not attractive or desirable enough to have the mate you want.

- The thought that you will never be financially secure or successful.

- The thought that you are doomed to a bad life because of your early upbringing and the mistakes you have made.

■ The thought that you are lazy, dumb, selfish, or bad.

■ The thought that you have to do everything a certain way—perfectly— to feel accomplished.

■ The thought that you will never achieve your dreams.

Once you've written down the mental junk words, begin to mentally discard them. Say to yourself, "I am throwing these junk thoughts into the trashcan where they belong." As you say this, crumple up the paper and throw it into an actual trashcan. You can also light the paper on fire (as long as it's not a fire hazard), and watch as the physical and mental junk burns—leaving your mind forever.

Samantha, an artist in her early-50s, was bitter about men. Her three previous partners had cheated on her and had treated her like trash. Although they seemed wonderful in the beginning, once their psychological masks came off, their true natures came out. They were cheaters, manipulators, and liars.

Yet, deep down, Samantha knew that not all men were like that. During therapy, she began to realize that she kept unconsciously attracting men like her father—a cheater who had abused her mother. Wanting to change her mental pattern, she wrote down the names of the men who had cheated on her, and put "Cheaters" in bold red ink on the paper. Then, she lit them on fire and threw them in a trash can as she repeated, "Goodbye cheaters. I will no longer pick men like you, like my father. I will choose men who are loyal, devoted, loving, and true—the type of man I deserve, to match the type of woman I am."

Feeling liberated and positive, Samantha started getting involved in social activities again. She loved cooking and started throwing food parties where friends could sample her tasty treats. She also started dating again and is optimistic that, this time, she will meet the type of partner who is right for her: a loving and loyal man who treats her with care and respect.

The good news is this: When you get rid of junk you are not really losing anything; you are actually gaining something of immense value.

You are clearing out your mental space so you can find the good things in life such as peace, compassion, and love that have been hidden under the junk all this time.

Think of how much true joy and pleasure you will experience once you find the hidden treasures—peace, goodwill, confidence, love— that have been inside you all along. By getting rid of the mental junk, you have added by subtraction. You have rid yourself of the pain, and you have transformed it into pure raw power to use for your own good and the good of others.

Use Failure to Grow Your Mental Muscles

Although it may sound counterintuitive, failure used rightly, can actually help you grow as a human being. The more you learn from your so-called failures or mistakes, the stronger you will become, and the better you will be able to overcome obstacles in the future.

Although few people intentionally pursue defeat, it's true that failure, when taken the right way, has a tremendous power to change your life for the good. In fact, you can think of failure as Inverted Power—it has the same power as success, only in a different direction. With the right mindset, you can reverse that energy to accomplish what you want. There are certain benefits to using defeat or pain to empower yourself to overcome obstacles and be more successful in life. For example, using defeat the right way can help you:

■ *Break your old bad habits and develop positive mental patterns.* Release energy for a fresh start with better habits: Finish what you start, be true to your word, eat healthy and exercise, and engage in a spiritual or relaxation practice.

■ *Take inventory of your assets and liabilities.* Write down your psychological strengths and weaknesses, and create an action plan for accentuating your assets and minimizing your liabilities. Perhaps, you are a good idea person, but a poor organizer. If that is the case, focus on coming up with more ideas, while striving to become better at organizing and implementing them (or find someone who can help you do it).

■ *Strengthen your willpower.* Challenge yourself to a greater effort to overcome an obstacle. When you feel like quitting on your self-development, tell yourself that you will give a little extra effort to see what happens. In this way, each small effort cumulatively builds up your confidence and motivation until you achieve your ultimate goals.

■ *Build Your Mental Muscles.* Think of defeat like resistance training in building muscles. In this type of training, you bring the weight down slowly. Every time you return it to where you started, you do so deliberately, concentrating on the process. You train yourself to get stronger each time.

In the same way, defeat can be like the weight you use. Each time you learn from defeat, you build stronger psychological muscles. Although there may be some initial growing pain, the pain turns into pleasure as you feel healthier and stronger after each workout. When you grow your mental muscles, you keep your mind so busy with desired circumstances that you have no time left to devote to undesired circumstances such as fears or frustrations.

From Poor Me to Blessed I

If you feel depressed about "Poor Me" (your suffering in life), simply reverse the energy and express gratitude to nature or God for all of the good things in life: love, romance, sex, friendship, babies, puppies, nature, music, creativity, laughter, and joy.

When you feel grateful for all that life has to offer, you move away from thoughts of self-preoccupation and move into a place of increased joy and enhanced compassion. You are happy regardless of the problems and obstacles you have to deal with because you know that you have plentiful resources to deal with them. You also have more concern for your family, friends, and even strangers. You care more about others because you have an overflow of goodwill and love as a result of your grateful way of looking at the world. You see all of the good that comes to you, and you rejoice on a daily basis.

Here's another defeat reversal technique: Find someone with a greater sorrow than yours and help them overcome it. Help a homeless person, console someone going through a breakup or divorce, offer company to a lonely elderly person. By doing this, you are demonstrating empathy—putting yourself in their shoes—as well as compassion: the desire to relieve their suffering.

One of the greatest things about helping others is that, by doing so, you are also helping yourself. Because you feel grateful for all of the resources you have—energy, time, money, joyfulness, and life itself—you feel that you have more than enough resources to help others, as well as yourself. You also see how all of us are connected to each other. We all suffer, we love, we grow, and we learn. It is a marvelous thing to be grateful for being part of the human race, and for our ability to help alleviate the suffering of others, just as we would want others to help us.

Also remember that no matter how much you have suffered in the past, you have vast undamaged areas in your mind. You have many parts of your mind that are still pure, fresh, and untouched by the pain of the past. Tap into these areas mentally by visualizing a fresh, clear stream of blue water, as you see yourself bathing in that water on a beautiful sunny day. Visualize that the water is cleansing you of any impurities and leaving you in a healthy and relaxed state of mind.

Walk in the Light and Live Free

Another way to increase your Mountain of Invincibility is to "Walk in the Light"—to live a kindhearted and truthful life in which you focus on spreading goodness in the world.

Let's study the phrase, "Walking in the Light," more deeply.

First of all, there is a distinction made between "Light" and "Darkness." Light, in the psychological and spiritual sense, refers to an upward path to truth, dignity, and love. It means that you live a life full of love, goodness, and contribution to the world. Light does not harm or hate; it builds, protects, and grows. Light is synonymous with love because love can shine light on the negative energies of life and remove its darkness.

Darkness, on the other hand, refers to hiding things, dishonesty, selfishness, violence, and even evil. Darkness seeks to push down, attack, and destroy the good. It can range from a personal darkness, such as yielding to a self-harming temptation, to a societal darkness: evil that revels in its darkness and leads to war, crime, prejudice, and moral destruction.

Seeking the light is an acknowledgement that you are looking to become a better, happier, loving, and more productive human being. The term "light" also applies to mates and life partners. Ideally, a couple in love would utilize this phrase when they ponder their purpose for being together. Their higher purpose is to be together, not solely for companionship, sex, or the creation of a family, but to "create light in the world." The light in a couple could refer to being good parents, neighbors, friends, or lovers of life. It could refer to creating a business or venture together that contributes to society or alleviates suffering. Whatever they do together, their purpose is to bring genuine truth and goodness to the earth.

Next, let's examine the importance of the term "walk" in the phrase, "Walk in the Light." Note that the term "talking about light," or "thinking about light" is not used. The word "walk" refers to taking an action and moving toward a certain direction.

There are plenty of people who talk a good game, but don't do anything to back up their words. They may talk a lot about goodness, peace, and love, but they don't demonstrate these virtues through their actions. In fact, they may do the opposite—showing anger while talking about love; demonstrating envy while professing empathy for others.

Things are different when you take daily action to walk in the light (or goodness) on the way to reaching your lasting state of Invincibility. More than mere idle chatter, you will take the necessary steps to move in the right direction of your inner growth.

Also, notice how the term "walk" refers to slow, leisurely progress. Here, the word "run" is not used. Walking is relaxed and patient. You place one foot in front of the other in a steady manner. Contrast the steady walking approach with the mad rush and frenzy of human beings in the large population areas of the world. In today's society, men and women frantically chase and run after each other, as well as after their ideas of what they think could make them happy—money, popularity, or material success.

On the other hand, the expert walker is never in a rush. They walk at a relaxed pace, and with pure awareness. They know where they are going, and they are conscious of each step they are taking. The expert walker is able to align their goals with their abilities and deal with obstacles when they meet them.

Janice and Tabitha, both in their mid-30s, had been friends since elementary school. They looked similar with red hair and freckles, and even had similar sounding voices. Yet they couldn't have been more different.

Tabitha, a systems analyst, had already been divorced three times, and was easily irritated by the "dumb people" in life—she thought she knew better than everyone else, and had moved from job to job trying to prove it. Although miserable and frustrated most of the time, she believed, deep down, that it was always someone else's fault. She was right and everyone else was wrong.

Her friend, Janice, on the other hand, was the polar opposite of Tabitha in temperament and maturity. Happily married with three children, she excelled in her job as a college professor, and was loved by students and friends alike. Quick with a smile and encouraging words, she always strove to improve herself and help others. Her motto was: "Love is the best investment you can ever make."

Although Janice tried to help Tabitha, suggesting self-help books and spirituality podcasts to give her friend a new perspective, Tabitha would become angry when Janice tried to help. In her mind, Tabitha already knew all the answers; she just needed people to "act right" and give her what she wanted. "One day," she thought, "I will get what I deserve."

Unfortunately, there are people like Tabitha who think they are walking in the light, but, in reality, are "running in the dark"—living with a sense of entitlement, trying to chase imaginary prizes, running away from unrealistic fears.

The good news is that you can learn how to Walk in the Light by applying the principles you are learning in this book. In the process, you will increase your compassion, confidence, and inner strength. As you become an expert psychological walker, you will realize that the light is a beautiful place to be—an oasis of peace, love, and happiness.

As you walk, you will understand that the journey itself is part of the oasis. Along the way, you will sample parts of the oasis as you journey toward your ultimate destination in life: Invincibility.

Although the road has its thorns (problems) and holes (setbacks), the beauty of the light (goodness and love) will keep you focused on the right path. It will give you the sustenance and protection you need for your marvelous journey to the best You.

Go Through the Pain Gap

As you learn to walk in the light, there will be times when you will be challenged by your Self-Defeating Mind. It will tell you that you don't have enough willpower to go through the Pain Gap: the gap between the way you are now—a person trapped by negative thoughts and feelings—and the way you want to be: a happy and healthy person with an Invincible Mind. When you go through the Pain Gap, you will experience some growing pains as you make the transition to a healthy and powerful mind.

For example, let's say that you have been surrounded by friends or family members who are gossipers and complainers. They seem to delight in criticizing you and making you feel bad. Although they may have provided you with a certain sense of security over the years, they have made you pay for it with their unrelenting negativity and criticism.

If you move away from them, physically or mentally, you may initially feel some nostalgia and insecurity (Pain Gap) because you have known them for a long time. However, you also realize that you will be better off without their negativity and self-defeating energies infiltrating your peace of mind. Once you cross the Pain Gap of harmful and negative people, you will be able to attract positive people and healthy relationships into your life.

Going through the Pain Gap is not just about leaving negative people behind; it also consists of saying "goodbye" to other negative and painful elements in your mind such as dark thoughts and compulsive behaviors that harm you: "the poor me" mentality, procrastination, self-doubt, bad habits, people and chemical addictions, giving up too early, and so on. Although these thoughts and actions are harmful for you, they are known to you. They can provide a false sense of comfort because you have been accustomed to them for a long time.

Many people are afraid to cross the "Pain Gap"—that momentary uncertain state in which they are between two worlds. On one end, is their old world dominated by the Self-Defeating Mind. On the other side, is the new world guided by The Invincible Mind.

Think of it this way: Imagine that the Pain Gap is like a river you must cross to get to a beautiful land of plenty and joy where you will discover positive and healing thoughts. You are presently on the ugly side of the river that is full of psychological weeds and creepy mental creatures: self-defeating thoughts, negative feelings, and unhappy experiences. All you have to do is wade across that shallow river until you get to the other side. There you will find lush vegetation and a fertile land full of positive emotions such as love and peace.

As you cross the river to your Invincible Mind, you will get closer to who you really are. The closer you get to the other side of the river, the better you will feel. You will sense that you are getting closer to your true destination: The real Invincible You.

Live Invincibly

As you're reading about how to increase your Mountain of Invincibility, you may be thinking to yourself, "I've tried to work on myself before and I failed. I fell back into my old negative ways: addictions, bad habits, harmful relationships, and unproductive mindsets."

Here's the answer to your problem: *Attempting Invincibility is beneficial even if you don't initially achieve it.*

Repeat this phrase to yourself several times: "Attempting Invincibility is beneficial even if I don't initially obtain it."

Simply trying to live a higher life is a great advantage because it clears your mind for new and higher thoughts. When you begin to work on your Invincible Mind, you transcend your previous stuck and negative self. You gain more motivation and desire to keep growing as a human being and improving your state of mind. Despite any drawbacks and obstacles, if you persist in working on your Invincible Mind, you will become stronger mentally and spiritually, and you will be able to fulfill your deepest dreams.

People give many excuses for not living an Invincible life. Here are some common reasons for not living Invincibly:

Excuse 1: "It's too hard to live this life of Invincibility."

Answer: Don't take the difficult as the impossible. Also realize that the more you work on yourself, the easier it becomes.

Excuse 2: "These higher-level ideas don't work on me."

Answer: How do you know until you have tried them?

The best evidence for whether these Invincible Mind principles work is to try them on yourself. Focus on becoming a How Thinker, exchanging mental trash for mental treasure, using failure to grow your mental muscles, walking in the light, and going through the Pain Gap.

Think of it as an experiment you will undertake for a certain period of time. There is nothing to lose. You can always go back to your old ways if you think the new approach is not working out. But, if it does work, think of what an amazing feeling you will experience—a constant state of joy, gratitude, and optimism.

Excuse 3: "I am too deep in my misery. I can't change."

Answer: Regardless of the mental or physical condition you are currently in, you can improve and grow. It has worked for many people, and it can work for you, too. Often, people become impatient in their inner development. They don't seem to see much change in their life; they complain they are getting nowhere.

The secret is to take one step, however small, toward your goal of Invincibility each day—exchange one self-defeating thought for a self-enhancing one; spend thirty minutes daily reading and listening to higher wisdom; take one small action toward an important project or dream you've been aiming for.

The good news is that, as you start to make progress toward your goal of Invincibility, you will become more patient, confident, compassionate, and grateful. You will also see other positive attributes and states of mind you can create. You will exchange negative mental states for positive ones, and you will transform your painful memories into useful life lessons. Soon, you will start to notice the changes in yourself happen—automatically and naturally.

Now, as you climb the mountain of your own power, you will no longer look back at the limiting mental desert of your past. You realize that the dry desert was never your home; the elevated and refreshing mountain was always your true dwelling place.

There, you will see the sun shining and the stars sparkling. You are moving to your permanent destination: The world of your Invincible Mind.

Soon, you will start to discard the negativity of the past for a new and exciting way of thinking and living. You will leave the mental desert and climb the beautiful mountain as you realize that the dry desert was never your home; the refreshing mountaintop was always your true dwelling place. There, you will find the sun shining and the stars sparkling.

Congratulations. You are now moving to a new permanent destination: The world of your Invincible Mind.

Chapter Thirteen

Center Yourself in the Hara

You have a great power which exists two inches below your navel. It is called the Hara—the center of your power and intuition.

In Eastern tradition, the Hara is the physical point that lies two inches below your navel and represents your life energy: your power, stability, balance, and intuition. In martial arts demonstrations, martial artists, no matter how big or small, can't be pushed from their position when they focus on their Hara. They are immovable and fixed in their point in space. They are said to be "in the Hara"—in the zone of ultimate balance, calmness, and power.

You can also see the Hara as your gut instinct, the part of you that knows what is right. Do you trust your gut instinct when it comes to relationships, finances, or important life decisions? If you don't, then you are likely to make more mistakes and slow down your life progress. If you do trust your gut, you are usually better able to make the right decisions and take the best actions.

The Hara is your true center of excellence. It is your awakened point of power. When you are in the Hara, you have a sense of being grounded, solid, in flow, and at ease. You say to yourself, "This feels like me, my true self." You have unhurried serenity, peace, and inner power, as opposed to being unhappy, uneasy, and strained.

When you act with full awareness of your Hara, the most trivial act becomes dynamic. Even brushing your teeth or combing your hair becomes an enjoyable experience with awareness. Making love, expressing your creative talent, or spending time with animals and children become acts of joy when you do them from your Hara, your inner core.

At the same time, when you live from your Hara, you can be in the center of a psychological storm with angry and difficult people, and be completely unaffected. The reason is that your nature is different from the storm. You are at a higher vantage point where the storm—the negativity of the outside world—can't affect you. You are removed from its damaging force because you reside in the Hara: a higher seat of power and intuition.

Just like you are able to master fear when you become aware of it, the Hara can help you become aware of the many different parts of your personality—the conflicting sides of you.

All of us have different sides. Sometimes, we are kind; other times rude; sometimes confident; sometimes timid. The best approach is to integrate all of these aspects as a whole and integrated self, which we call the Hara.

In this chapter, you will learn how to tap into the force of your psychological Hara, your inner stability and rock-solid mental power. Known as resiliency in the West, and Hara power in the East, the Hara is an important concept you need to internalize if you are to withstand the pressures of life and attain the true success and happiness you desire.

But, before we explore the power of the Hara, let's examine what happens when a person is unbalanced and not connected to their Hara—when they are self-divided and untrue to their inner nature.

The "I'm Sorry" Woman

Once there was a woman who apologized to everyone. If she didn't buy something at a store, she said, "I'm sorry; it's outside my budget." If a friend wanted too much time from her, she would say, "I'm sorry; I wish I had more time."

She even apologized for apologizing too much.

She had grown up in a family where nothing she did was ever right. She was constantly criticized by her parents: "You don't do anything right. You're always screwing up." As a result, she got into the habit of saying, "I'm sorry" for the things she did wrong—which she felt applied to almost everything she did.

As an adult, her apologetic and fearful nature continued as she apologized to her friends and work colleagues, and even strangers. Then one day, a friend gave her powerful advice: "Don't apologize to anyone. Just be yourself, and you will be OK."

As she thought about it further, she realized that her apologies only served to weaken her and didn't help her relationships—others saw her as someone to be taken advantage of. Slowly, she began to overcome her need to apologize.

Although in the beginning she was tempted to say, "I'm sorry," she began to hold back her need to defend or explain herself. Eventually, she became a new person. Free of the need to apologize, she realized she could be genuinely compassionate and caring, starting with herself.

When you are self-divided, and not in tune with your true nature, you have a forced and apologetic air about you. You laugh at jokes that aren't really funny to you; you express concern for things that you don't truly care about. Or, you do the opposite. You take an argumentative stance and try to prove you are right, and everyone else is wrong, because you don't feel valuable enough as you are.

Whether you are a people-pleaser or argumentative, the problem is that you may believe that others have more value than you—consequently, you work overly hard to try to please them or to prove yourself right in their eyes—often at the cost of your own authenticity and peace of mind. Because you are presenting a false self to others, either overly agreeable or overly combative, you are not being your true self—and it hurts.

When you are self-divided or inauthentic, you are always tired. Although you may actually have a lot of natural physical energy, you also carry energy-robbing and unnecessary mental burdens: blame, guilt, self-pity, and sorrow.

On the other hand, when you live from your Hara, your true self, you don't need to apologize to anyone for anything. You are living in love, which means you can't be hurt, and you can't hurt anyone. You live an authentic life.

Self-Unity is Your Success

To access the power of your Hara, your center, you need self-unity. Self-unity exists when your inner and outer life are the same: When you talk of peace and have peace; when you talk of love and have love.

Many of us know people who appear to be unified, but really aren't. They have conflicting parts of themselves that diminish their credibility.

Some people angrily tell you they are compassionate. Others sneakily try to convince you they are trustworthy. In either case, they are not unified. They are presenting a façade which hides the opposite trait.

You might ask: "How can a person perform a good act one minute, but then be unkind the next?"

The answer is that they have "Divided Goodness." When wanting a reward, a person can perform a good act without having a good nature. They are self-divided. Their next act will be harmful. Only an undivided person—one who has singleness of mind—is truly good. Their actions will be natural and effortless. A flower easily gives out perfume because it is a flower.

In the same way, a self-unified person is whole and complete. They are happy, self-sufficient, and content within themselves.

For the unified person, there is no division—nothing hidden; nothing contradictory. A self-unified individual doesn't just talk about being a good person; they show their goodness through example. They do so by helping others without asking for credit; by being patient when everything around them is a madhouse; by giving when there is nothing for them to gain.

How do you become unified as a human being? By doing what is truly you—engaging with the people and activities that resonate with your authentic nature.

If you want to start a business to change the world, that is your calling. If you want to raise children to be happy and healthy human beings, then that is your grand mission. If you simply want to be a kind, loving, and compassionate person—without any unique or great career goals—then, again, that is your nature, and who you were meant to be.

Always ask yourself: "Is this right for me? Do I feel good in my gut about this person, situation, or decision?" If the answer is "Yes," then pursue it. If the answer is "No," then move in a different direction. Many times, we know what is right for us, but we choose to ignore our intuition. We get into the wrong relationship, unhealthy lifestyle choice, or losing money-making proposition because we don't listen to our Hara, our gut.

This is not to say that we must blindly go with every deep feeling we have about something. We can also investigate, research, and look at the facts in an analytical and practical way. Yet, once we have gathered all of the data, and we're still not sure about our decision, relying on our intuition is often our best choice. Our Hara can lead us where we need to go.

Because self-unity is so important to your happiness and well-being, it's good for you to have as much of it as you can.

Exercise: Live Authentically This Week

Here's an experiment you can try:

Live the unified and authentic life and see what happens. Decide that this week you will go for what is truly authentic to you from your Hara (your gut).

You will say what you really feel; you will interact with people you really want to be with (not due to obligation or loneliness), and you will pursue the activities that bring you true pleasure. This week you will experiment with doing what is natural for you, and you will see the difference it makes in your life.

For example, you may get along with a certain person naturally and enjoy their company, even though they are not your usual "type" (physically or psychologically). If that is the case, experiment and see if you can create a friendship or relationship with this individual. You may be surprised at how well you can get along with them because you resonate on the same level.

On the other hand, you may feel stressed or pressured when you're with another person who, on the surface, appears to be your type. When you're with them, you may feel like you have to play a role; you have to be someone you're not, and it makes you uneasy. If that's the case, then you may need to reconsider whether you want to spend a lot of time with this person. The relationship may not be authentic or harmonious.

At first, you may find it difficult to step out of your comfort zone and go against your customary choices in choosing people or situations that may seem attractive or exciting at first glance, but are not really good for you in the long run. That physically attractive person who lacks depth or commitment; that potentially "get rich quick" business or financial opportunity that doesn't quite feel right. But, as you start to focus on your authenticity—and the truth of your Hara—you will begin to see life in reverse. What you thought was superficially attractive or appealing may actually be quite ugly once you examine it closer; what you thought wasn't that alluring can actually possess true beauty at its core.

Here's the truth: There is nothing more beautiful than self-unity. You can choose today to live from your unified and authentic nature, your true Hara. You can select the people and situations that resonate with who you really are; with what you truly desire, deep down. When you do this, you will be happier and healthier, and you will be able to accomplish much more.

One-Point Hara Focus: Concentrated Power

Your one-point Hara focus refers to maintaining complete and utter concentration on your primary focus or mission in life. It means being guided by your Hara (gut or instinct) and maintaining a laser-like focus on what you want to accomplish.

In this mindset, you refuse to be distracted by anything else that is not your purpose. You will only focus your eyes straight ahead to your aim—not looking to the left, nor to the right.

When you have one-point focus, you unleash tremendous power to achieve your desires. In this approach, your life is concentrated and free from distractions. Individuality is only successful when it is concentrated. When you focus on developing your unique talent or ability (Don), you will have more confidence and satisfaction because you are good at what you do.

At the same time, you won't waste as much time on things that could distract you from expressing your talent and helping others. These include mind-numbing news, excessive use of smart phones, tablets and video games; flashy, but superficial activities and people, and trivial conversations and gossip.

Although there's nothing wrong with partaking in entertainment and minor distractions in small doses as a change of pace from other activities, your main focus will be different. You will concentrate on doing what you do best, and what you enjoy the most; whether it is teaching, science, spirituality, crafts, the arts, sports, mechanics, family and domestic life, or business.

Moreover, you won't try to be good at something you're not interested in. For example, a person who doesn't like school may decide they are better off starting their own business instead of going to college. Another individual may want to obtain additional years of graduate school training because they love the academic world.

Regardless of which route they take, the one-point Hara focused person has decided to concentrate on the one thing, or things, they love the most. Consequently, they withdraw themselves from thoughts, discussions, and activities that are better carried out by others. They don't waste time on things they only *pretend* to have an interest in. Instead of talking to the person standing next to the one they are really interested in, they talk directly to the one they want to meet. Instead of wasting time in an unfulfilling job, they focus their energies on transitioning to their dream career or profession.

Start today to focus on those areas in your life in which you are unique—where you stand out; where you feel the most energized and powerful. Express your true identity in everything you do. If you have a talent for numbers, work with them. If your gift is speaking, exercise your verbal muscles. If writing is your thing, put your thoughts into written words. If caring for others is your talent, focus on helping people.

To maintain your one-point focus, spend time with people who truly support what you are doing. It's much easier to maintain your Hara focus when you have people around you who encourage and believe in you. Although it's good to be self-motivated, sharing your successes with appreciative people can raise your desire to reach your goal. It can increase your momentum toward winning the prize you're aiming for.

Another good Hara development strategy is to simplify things and get to the core of the matter. If you're a business person, for example, try this: Before your next business meeting or phone call, clarify the exact purpose for the interaction. Type one or two words on your tablet or computer regarding what the conversation is going to be about.

For example, "Close deal." "Get parameters." "Create relationship."

After you initially engage in small talk to establish rapport, you will maintain your one-point focus at the forefront of your mind: the mission or purpose for the phone call or meeting. While observing the niceties of human connection, you will also be primarily focused on accomplishing your chief objective, whether it's to get more information, make a deal, and so forth.

When you go straight to the essence of every conversation and situation, you will live fully from your Hara. You will flow with life, and you will get better results in a more efficient manner.

Hara Focus Secrets

Here are some simple strategies for attaining one-point Hara focus and achieving ultimate success:

■ *Associate with people who are calm and controlled; patient and understanding.* Spend time with those who have an unrelenting focus and desire to do good.

■ *Don't spend a great deal of time and energy on catastrophic or sensational stories seen on TV or the Internet,* such as the ones involving famous people behaving badly, political scandals, or stories of senseless violence. The sheer repetition of horrible deeds and human suffering can overwhelm your emotional faculties and weaken your powers of concentration.

■ *Make every action you take a purposeful one that is designed to achieve your highest objective.* Talk to the people you need to talk to, invest time, energy, and money in the thing that yields the greatest result or benefit; plan daily and execute your plan.

■ *Calm your nervous energy.* If you get overly excited or nervous, you may use up your vital energies—making it difficult for you to focus on what you need to accomplish. Calm yourself down by taking a walk in nature, exercising, meditating, or engaging in a spiritual practice. Relaxing your mind like this can help you come up with new solutions and put your problems in perspective.

■ *Concentrate on your successes:* Think of how you have succeeded in the past and can do so again.

■ *Be fully immersed in whatever you are doing in the moment.* Whether you're eating, engaging in a leisure activity, or working on a project, make sure you maintain full awareness of what you're doing in the present moment.

This last point is important. Instead of thinking about the thousand things you have to do, focus only on the one thing you are doing right now.

When you are engaged in pleasure or relaxation, fully experience it. When you are involved in work, fully experience it. Don't try to commingle the two, thinking of play when you're working, or thinking of work when you're playing. If you do that, you will weaken your emotional and psychological forces, and you will enjoy neither one.

Apply the same principle of concentration in your daily encounters with people. When you shake someone's hand, imagine that your hand contains hundreds of individual loving minds, each having an intelligence of its own. When you put feeling into a handshake, it shows your personality; it's an expression of your loving energy. This hand of love offers warmth and comfort to the person you're interacting with and draws them closer to you. Practice giving a warm and steady handshake to others, and you will see how people are attracted to you because of the charisma you project.

Also, breathe deeply when you are happy, and you will gain more strength and energy because you will associate breathing—the essence of living—with happy emotions. As you inhale, you will feel the power of being alive, and you will experience positive feelings such as gratitude, optimism, and love.

In the end, your daily goal is to think the deepest thoughts of Invincibility—to completely kill your belief in your limitations—to drive away all fear and destructive thought forces. Instead of suffering under the burden of negative thoughts, you will build a strong assurance that every venture you engage in will be successful.

By concentrating your forces and attacking at the point where you may achieve a breakthrough, you can defeat the feelings of futility, deprivation, and being overwhelmed. You will gain inner power and the belief that you can, indeed, accomplish your deepest dreams.

For example, if you are good at verbal skills, but not so good at writing, then gear your daily activities to your strength—verbal interactions. The opposite is true if you are a better writer than speaker; to perfect your craft, spend more time writing than speaking. Another possibility is that you may have a passion for something that you are not naturally talented at, but your drive and hard work ethic can help you become very good at it. In either case, your goal is to use whatever ability or talent you have to help yourself and those around you.

Here are some useful questions for building your Hara, your essential nature:

- *How would you behave toward others if you realized their powerlessness to hurt you?* Behave like that.

- *How would you react to so-called misfortune if you saw its inability to bother you?* React like that.

- *How would you think toward yourself if you knew you were alright?* Think like that.

By asking these questions, and answering them in the right way, you will maintain singleness of mind. You will be in touch with your energetic center because you are eliminating the extraneous things from your life such as worry and self-doubt. Instead of focusing on your weaknesses and limitations, you are concentrating on your abilities and power to make a difference in the world.

Create a Hara Focus Statement

A good way to concentrate on what you truly want is to create a Hara Focus Statement. This is a simple phrase or sentence that summarizes what you want out of life. Write it down or type it in your tablet or computer. Read it daily.

Here are some of the Hara Focus Statements of great achievers from history:

Abraham Lincoln: "Free the slaves."
Martin Luther King, Jr.: "Bring equality, respect, and civil rights to all humans."

Mother Teresa: "Feed the poor of the world."
Thomas Edison: "Harmonize natural laws for the good of humanity."
Steven Jobs: "Think different."
Florence Nightingale: "Heal the sick with compassion."

When you focus on your Hara statement—a life-driving mission or purpose—you liberate your energies and increase your motivation to reach your dreams. You plan better, work harder, and recover more quickly from setbacks. You learn that each setback, or "failure," you experience on the way to your goal has within it the seed of a great benefit. Each lesson learned, each strength developed, will bring you one step closer to your goal.

EXERCISE: ANCHOR YOURSELF TO YOUR IMMOVABLE HARA

Ask a friend to help you with the following exercise:

Stand with your feet shoulder length apart and bend your knees. Now, visualize that a steel rod is extending from the ground and connecting to your Hara—two inches below the navel. Imagine that this steel rod is anchoring you firmly to the ground so that nothing can move or disturb you.

Now, have your friend lightly apply pressure on your chest with their palm as you feel the stability and firmness in your posture. Gradually, they can apply more pressure as you continue to visualize yourself standing rock solid in your position—nothing can move or shake you.

As you practice this exercise, you may be surprised at how much force and pressure you can resist (without moving or being knocked off balance) when you are grounded in your Hara, your center of power and intuition. In daily life, when you face pressures and stresses from the environment, as well as difficult people, imagine that a steel rod is connecting your Hara to the ground so that nothing can push you off balance or bother you. When you are grounded in your Hara like this, you are calm, relaxed, and powerful in what you believe in and what you want to do. You are immovable; you are Invincible.

The Hara as Your Centerpoint

In the East, the Hara is identified as the point of physical balance and equilibrium—represented by a point two inches below your navel. From a psychological perspective, the Hara can be seen as your emotional and spiritual point of balance, also known as your Centerpoint.

The Centerpoint represents the balance, or midpoint, between different states of life and mind. Between arrogance and self-doubt, there is confidence. Between aggression and submission, there is self-respect. Between sadness and happiness, there is maturity. We need the Centerpoint, but we also need the two sides at either extreme.

Without sadness, we wouldn't know what joy is. Without cold, we wouldn't appreciate the comfort of warmth. Without darkness, we wouldn't bask in the light. Without thirst, water wouldn't be so joyfully received.

To live from the Hara, your centered self, is to stand in the middle of life, while extending yourself in both directions simultaneously. You feel compassion for the sadness of others; you feel the joy that others experience. You see where anger has its place; you see where peace can heal wounds. If you look at the other side of disappointment, you will find its opposite, "Fulfilled Expectations." You see that if you have great expectations, you may have great disappointments, but also great fulfillments of your goals and desires. If you have small expectations, you may have little disappointments, but also little fulfillments.

With the Centerpoint perspective, you see that each side has its advantages and disadvantages. You are able to have the best of both worlds as you stand in the middle and extend your energy toward both dimensions.

One great advantage of living in the Centerpoint is that time ceases to have its powerful and fearful hold over you. You no longer have the thought that you are running out of time and have wasted your life. You recognize that the now, the present moment you are experiencing, is the midpoint between the "before" and the "after." You see the beauty of the past and the hope of the future.

And, by maintaining your full awareness on the moment, you realize that you *are* the past, and you *are* the future. This is true because your mind contains the remnants of the past as well as the seeds of the future. In between, you live fully in the present—the rich, juicy moments of now. You are like the Samurai Warrior who is so centered that he senses anyone approaching him from all directions, even at a distance.

To find your center, you need to be grounded in your Hara. You need to act from your gut, your intuition, by doing the things you feel are right for you; whether they involve your relationships, finances, career, or personal issues.

When you are grounded in your Hara, you are able to reclaim all of the hidden parts of you—the ugly, awkward, and self-defeating parts, as well as the beautiful, gracious, and loving sides. By bringing home all of the parts of yourself that you have projected onto the environment, you take ownership of who you really are—you become the ruler of your body, mind, and soul.

Although there is great potential inside you right now, chances are you may have some kind of blockage—perhaps, fear, regret, or self-doubt—that is preventing you from expressing your fullest and most powerful nature.

Consider a therapy patient who is confused and torn between two parts of themselves. Part of them wants to be easy-going and loving to others. The other part wants to be tough and strong—to stand up to people who try to take advantage of them.

To begin the process of healing, they need to fully identify with both parts of themselves—the easy-going part and the tough part. They can take turns playing the strong role, and then the easy-going, pleasing persona in daily life situations. At times, they will practice speaking plainly and bluntly—stating what they want directly, using statements instead of questions, and maintaining a poker face and direct eye contact. Other times, they will smile more, be more pleasant and agreeable, and strive to achieve harmony in the interaction.

Recognizing that each style has its unique advantages and disadvantages, the person will practice playing both roles, eventually entering into a rhythm of their own uniqueness. They can learn to be a "people person" when the occasion calls for it, and when to go against the prevailing opinion and speak their mind directly and bluntly. By allowing their inner polar opposites to exist, they restore their lost energy which was misspent fighting external circumstances such as trying to be liked, or in charge of others.

You can benefit from the same type of unity by deciding to integrate the different and opposing parts of your personality—shy and outgoing; tough-minded and sensitive; structured and spontaneous. When you do this, you access your different strengths, and you become a more powerful and balanced person.

Refresh Yourself in the Energy Pool

A good way to maintain Hara balance is to tap into the Refreshment of the Energy Pool, the store of emotional energy you have for different tasks and life activities.

Think of yourself as being surrounded by small pools of different specific energies: emotional, mental, sexual, social, and physical. Each day you draw from each pool as you feel the need. For example, you draw on social energy to have a good time at a party. Or, you draw on work energy to perform well on the job.

The well-balanced Invincible Mind person has plenty of energy to do what they wish. They recognize that to have sufficient energy pools, they need to have inner unity first. They need to think and act how they really feel. By doing so, they remove the psychological covers on the pools, and they have tremendous energy at their disposal that was previously contained. This Invincible person recognizes that it is useless to try to create energy by artificial means like trying to be funny or likeable at a social event if they don't feel like doing so. Only by being authentic will they release sufficient energy based on the situation.

At the same time, the Invincible person doesn't try to force the energy pools. When you're tired of doing a certain activity, it means that you have temporarily used up that particular pool of energy. At this point, you can go along with the natural flow of things to a different activity, which calls upon another pool—permitting the previous pool to refresh itself.

For example, when you're tired of something mental, do something physical such as exercising or cleaning house. When you're tired of the physical, do something mental, perhaps crossword puzzles, reading, or thinking. When you're tired of entertainment that exhausts your emotions, partake in a soothing or relaxing activity. Take a walk in nature; play with animals or children; take a warm bath. When you have run out of options, and have nothing to turn to, draw from the pool of faith or inspiration from a higher source, or drink from the well of perseverance from your own soul.

The key is to live a life of alternating effort and relaxation. You don't have to drive yourself all of the time. It's OK to have a change of pace. There are times when you get weary; when you feel discouraged and futile, and there are times when you have a lot of energy. When you feel down, don't be discouraged. Set your work aside. Have a tasty snack, some entertainment, physical exercise, or social diversion. When you're refreshed, you can come back and have double the energy to pick up where you left off.

The beautiful thing about the energy pool is that you don't need to think about changing activities. It happens by itself when the natural pool is exhausted. You just need to be aware of, and follow, the signal that is telling you to drop one activity and begin another. A hard-working businessperson can put aside their intense nature and goof off for a while without feeling lazy. An exhausted mom can take a break from the children and get herself a massage or facial without feeling guilty. As you spontaneously move from one activity to another in the energy pool of life, you will come to an amazing realization:

You are letting your life be lived through you.

You are no longer forcing things—trying to make people like you—or trying to capture that elusive good luck in finances, health, or love. Instead, you are harmonizing and flowing with what life, or reality, has to offer—you are enjoying the beauty of the present moment.

With this new way of living, you don't need luck: You *are* luck and everything else you need: love, happiness, and success.

The Unification of You

As you start to live more from your Hara and your Invincible Mind, you will see that true happiness has no beginning and no end. It is always there, ready for your realization.

As you become a unified human being, your outer speech will reflect your inner self. You will find that you talk in a more relaxed, soothing, and clear tone of voice.

It's true that your voice reveals your inner nature: The frightened person shows alarm in their speech; a critical person reveals their unkind nature in their words. Similarly, an inwardly composed person will be regal and gracious in their way of talking.

As an exercise on a daily basis, notice your speech habits: Do you speak high, low, fast, slow, or staccato? Do you have any filler words that you repeat often ("You know," "I mean" "Ah," "Uh-huh")? Do you wait patiently or impatiently for others to stop speaking?

Strive to maintain a calm, loving, and even temperament and vocal style centered in your Hara. Observe how your speech and mannerisms correspond to your united and balanced nature. When you walk in a room, strive to let your inner essence act for you. In everything you do, aim to represent your true self. Let your Hara nature be present— the part of you that is perfectly balanced, and in control; the powerful and loving essence within you that handles every challenge perfectly.

The lovely truth is that self-command dissolves all that is not yourself. Then, you can be who you really are: A free and loving human being.

Chapter Fourteen

Your Invincibility Blueprint

What does it take to be Invincible? It takes a commitment to grow yourself into the best person you can possibly be: smart, strong, compassionate, courageous, creative, and loving.

To do this, you need to design your Invincibility Blueprint, a formula for building your psychological resources with happy and positive emotions. On a daily basis, you will increase your creativity, patience, compassion, confidence, optimism, and love.

In everyday life, we have blueprints for our day. We have schedules, recipes, and standard ways of doing business and taking care of chores. However, few people have an Invincibility Blueprint—a detailed plan for inner and outer excellence that consists of developing positive habits, thoughts, and emotions to rewire your brain and bring you maximum results.

When you activate your Invincibility Blueprint, you gain psychological perspective. You learn how to distinguish between important things, such as love and learning, and unimportant matters like momentary slights and setbacks. You focus on the positive aspects of life while also learning how to overcome obstacles and problems. In the process, you become stronger and wiser. You build the wonderful quality known as Resilience—the ability to bounce back from momentary setbacks and defeats. The more resilient and Invincible you become, the more confidence you will have to continue growing and helping others grow as well.

Here are some techniques and exercises to help you create your personal Invincibility Blueprint:

Do One Right Act

To increase your Invincibility, begin by doing one small right act on your behalf. Make it as small as you want—just do that one right act.

If you're timid in front of someone, resolve that you will look them in the eye, just this one time.

If you have a habit of procrastinating, agree with yourself that you will start the project one day earlier than you normally would.

If you're afraid to take a risk in a financial opportunity, start by investing in a small way as you gain experience and confidence.

By doing this one small right act, you will gather momentum and energy. You begin to eradicate other problems that are tied to the first problem you are dealing with. If you master procrastination, you can also reduce your self-critical nature—you begin to forgive yourself when you are less than perfect. If you diminish your shyness in personal relationships, you can increase your confidence in speaking up at work.

In truth, genius is nothing more than doing the little things until they are done well enough to open the door of opportunity to greater things. When you do small things well, you build momentum and confidence. Each small accomplishment builds upon the next. Even setbacks, those so-called failures, add more fuel to the fire of your personal growth because you learn what *not* to do—thereby accelerating your progress and giving you a clearer vision of what you need to do to ultimately succeed.

To accelerate your growth, begin by building up your decision-making power. Decide quickly on small things. Instead of procrastinating, and putting things off for later, decide what you want to do and act quickly. Decide what you're going to say to a troublesome friend, where you're going on vacation, or what kind of gym you want to join. After you do your research, and have the facts you need, make your decision quickly.

Most of the time, the fear of making a mistake is what keeps you from acting decisively. However, the truth is that when you act quickly and intelligently, you will usually make fewer mistakes than if you were to delay and overthink things. When you act from your Hara or inner intuition, you find yourself making good choices as you move quicker toward the goals you want to accomplish.

Once you start succeeding with small aspects of your life, it's time to tackle the bigger issues and problems so you can create ingrained positive habits that lead you to success.

It's time to become a Mental Pathmaker.

Be a Mental Pathmaker

Would you like a shortcut to excellence? You can find it by becoming a Mental Pathmaker—a successful person who creates new habits through repetition. Each time you repeat the same desirable habit, you make the mental path (mental connections to the habit) deeper and wider. It becomes easier for you to do the things you want to do.

Let's say that you want to lose weight and get in shape. Of course, there will be resistance, i.e. your old ingrained habits. Your Self-Defeating Mind will tell you that it's too much work to lose weight. It will insist that your genetic makeup is not geared for you to do so. It will tell you, "Eat and be happy—let others worry about diet and exercise."

To become a Mental Pathmaker, and bypass the nagging thoughts of self-defeat, it's a good idea to start small. Begin by going to the gym for a short period of time each day. Gradually, you will get used to going to the gym, and you will increase the time you spend there—from 20 minutes to 30 minutes, to one hour or more. Pretty soon, you are feeling so good that you decide to take better care of your overall health. You eat better, quit smoking or excessive drinking, and sleep better. Your mental pathway of good health has become ingrained in your mind.

It is said that half the battle of achieving a goal is showing up—at the gym, a job interview, or on a date. Many people procrastinate and allow laziness, or the fear of failure, to take over. They don't make the effort to show up and take a beneficial action—working out, getting a job, creating a relationship—that could make a positive impact on their lives.

You will be different. You will create mental pathways by actually showing up at the place you need to be. If you want to get in shape, you will go the gym regularly. As you ingrain into your mind the idea that you will go to the gym at a specific time, you will find it easier to extend your time there and keep improving your workout to meet your health and appearance goals.

Decide that you will travel over newly made paths, e.g. your new exercise habits, as often as possible. The more often you go over the new paths, the sooner they will become comfortable for you, and the more you will enjoy your journey of self-development.

As you make upward strides toward your Invincibility, it's important that you keep your eyes forward on your improvement and the new path.

When you do this, the old negative path—not exercising—will try to lure you back. The old path will whisper in your mind, "Look at what you're missing out on. Remember all the fun we used to have eating junk food and just lying around the house watching TV." However, as you make more progress along the Invincible path, you will realize that the older path, the unhealthy lifestyle, wasn't really all that much fun. Apart from an initial small burst of pleasure, there was a significant amount of pain: regret, weakness, and diminished health and appearance.

There is good news. Once you burst through the initial resistance of staying the same, you will initiate a positive new "mental path." In the case mentioned above, you will change your eating and workout habits, and you will stick to a disciplined regimen. As a result, you will be healthier and happier.

By immersing yourself in your new healthy path, you will find that you are gaining more knowledge, experience, and confidence. You see that each successful action is cumulative. One success builds upon the next.

Bypass the Contraction Mindset

As you grow your Invincibility, you will find an obstacle in your way called the Contraction Mindset.

The Contraction Mindset occurs when your life energy gets weaker and smaller, and you are swept away by negative emotions such as anger, sadness, or regret. In this mental state, you are said to have Contracted Energy—your energy is withdrawing and diminishing. You feel weak, frustrated, and inadequate.

Contracted Energy comes in various forms.

First, there is anger, when you are feeling small and vulnerable, and you try to compensate for it by forming angry feelings inside you—lashing out at others for perceived slights or disrespect they have displayed toward you.

In another form of Contracted Energy, you are swept away by regret—you lament the things you could have done better. Perhaps, you regret the way you raised your children. You feel bad that you didn't give them enough time because you were too busy working. Or, you chastise yourself for staying in an incompatible or abusive relationship for too long for the sake of the kids (and they ended up suffering as well).

In yet another form, Contracted Energy sinks you into a state of profound sadness. You have lost the essential joy of living; you don't enjoy anything anymore. This sadness is also manifested in your physical expressions. Your body posture is slumped, your face loses its coloring, and your voice lacks spark and enthusiasm.

One example of Contracted Energy is what happens when someone suffers a trauma: a loss or painful experience. When this happens, the trauma becomes an ingrained part of their mind. The person begins to avoid situations, places, and people that trigger memories or flashbacks (reenactments) of the trauma.

For example, a person who was a victim of domestic abuse relives the physical and verbal attacks of her domestic partner whenever she passes by the kitchen of their house where many of the arguments occurred. She cringes when she touches the pot; she remembers the time her partner threw it at her. She has an angry and shocked feeling every time she looks at her phone—she recalls how she discovered her partner's many infidelities.

These mental intrusions—parasites of the mind—become embedded into the abused person's everyday consciousness. Moreover, the most recent trauma can activate a chain of memories of previous traumas such as child abuse, accidents, or abuse by a previous domestic partner.

In time, the memories of the trauma become the central point of their life. The traumatized person ignores other pleasurable things and focuses solely on the pain and horror of the abuse and trauma they suffered. The Energy Contraction continues. They start avoiding people and social interactions; they become depressed, sullen, and withdrawn. Their life is narrowing significantly.

The solution for the traumatized person is to expand their life energy and enlarge their inner and outer nature. To do this, they need to integrate the past trauma(s) into their lives. They need to come to peace with their past painful experiences. They do this by adopting the trauma as a part of their life that, although painful at the time, can also be a healing and life-affirming force. When they do this, they have learned something—they have found meaning; they have become stronger.

The Mother Who Transformed Her Love

Raul was returning home from college across country and was seeing his mother, Esperanza, after several years away. On the night of his arrival, he went out with some friends to celebrate. He saw a girl he liked and made an innocent comment, which she misinterpreted as a vulgar insult. Soon, she brought back several of her family members—armed with knives and bats— and they proceeded to stab and beat the young man to death.

When Esperanza found out that Raul, her only son, had been murdered, she was inconsolable. Months passed, and she still cried every day at the senseless murder of her beautiful boy.

As she underwent counseling, she struggled with her feelings of sadness, remorse, and anger. She even had a desire for vengeance against the perpetrators.

Slowly, Esperanza began to heal, and eventually discovered that she had a great yearning to be a foster mother for children without parents. She was a natural caretaker who loved children.

After a while, Esperanza became a foster mother, and in doing so, was able to recover some of her joy for living. She had lost a son who could never be replaced. However, in her pain, she was able to discover her true calling—to be a loving caregiver for children without parents. She could express the love she had for her son through the children she took care of.

Although a trauma invariably brings pain, the mother in this case made some good come from it. She expanded her awareness and love of life as a result of the trauma she experienced.

In the same way, when you experience pain, trauma, or defeat, you can look for the meaning or lesson in the pain. This lesson can help you reverse the tendency to withdraw or contract your energy, and can give you a new vehicle to expand your energy for the good of yourself and others.

Expand Your Mindset

With an Expansion Mindset, you are always looking to grow and contribute—you want to improve yourself and help others better themselves as well. You see life as an ever-increasing miracle of opportunities to experience, love, and learn.

When your mind is expanding, and you are thinking more positive and healthy thoughts every day, you are energetic, calm, and bright. You enjoy everything: food tastes better, stars shine brighter, birds sing more melodically. Overall, you see the world in an entirely different and positive light. Life becomes a joy for you.

In the East, your life energy is referred to as "Ki" energy. Your Ki is either getting bigger and expanding, bringing you more love, success, and happiness, or it is contracting—making you feel lethargic, aimless, and tired. Your goal is to expand your positive energy every day so you can become more joyful and mentally strong.

How do you expand your positive energy and mindset?

Listen to others with an attentive ear; help those who need it; resolve to be a kinder, more patient, and more loving person. Take courses or read materials about subjects that interest or fascinate you. Indulge your curiosity for experiencing new things, learning, and traveling. Take up a new hobby. Constantly work on your mind to become the person you truly want to be.

The paradox is that the very use of energy for mind expansion actually brings you more energy. This is true because the natural and inherent impulse of life is to seek to live more. It is the nature of intelligence to enlarge itself; it is the principle of consciousness to extend its boundaries to find fuller expression. The more you reach out to others and live in a positive way—both mentally and physically—the more your energy and power grows.

In the same way, we can apply the lesson of extending or withdrawing energy to the area of mental health. For example, a person who is under the influence of depression has contracted energy. They are wrapped up in their own self-contained mindset of negativity. Consequently, they lose touch with the outside world—even small, unimportant things become matters of great urgency and worry.

The cure for the depressed person is to extend their energy into the Universe—to expand (give, help, offer, learn), instead of contract. When they do this, they put themselves in a position in which good things can happen to them.

Use the Expansion Mindset to Handle Difficult People

Although expansion is the ideal way to live, it is not always easy, especially when you are surrounded by angry or difficult people. The critical and aggressive person's contracting energy can detonate an emotional bomb that explodes on you. What you need to do in this case is to expand your own energy to fill in the gap left by their contraction of energy.

By expanding your own energy—smiling, looking at the person in the eye, even agreeing with some of what they are saying—you defuse their aggression. Your goal is first to match their aggressive energy—not by being aggressive yourself—but by raising your tone of voice to match their intensity, while at the same time maintaining the softness of your words.

Let's say you have a conversation like this:

Irritated Person: "You're an idiot. You don't understand," (said in a loud, obnoxious voice).

You: "I have love for you as a human being, even though we have different views. You're angry right now. I can see that." You say this in a similarly loud voice; maybe just a notch lower in intensity. Although your voice is loud, and matches the intensity of the other person, your words are soft—creating a paradoxical effect that throws the angry person off guard. You have surprised the angry person and interrupted their hostile pattern. You have matched their vocal intensity; thereby showing them that you are not a pushover or weak. At the same time, you have responded with loving and kind words that lead to energy expansion.

This paradox of strength with softness will likely jolt them out of their self-hypnosis of being under the influence of the Anger Weakness. Consequently, you can open the door to honest communication.

When you match them in energy intensity, and then lead them into a place of peace and nonaggression, you are not being insincere or manipulative. Rather, you are expanding your energy to create a harmonious alliance with your energy-contracting conversational partner. When you do this, they will likely reduce their anger intensity since your positive energy has softened their negative energy. Moreover, your loving energy has filled the gap left by their anger energy. Remember that the greatest love is to transform your inner life so others are attracted by your genuine example of goodness.

Of course, not everyone will respond well to your energy expansion. But those who do may start to make changes in their lives to model the loving energy you are extending to them. In the end, the truth will be clear:

Love has no fixed point. It flows unceasingly; covering everything along the way.

Develop the Blast Off Mentality

Another way to skyrocket your progress into Invincibility is to develop the "Blast Off Mentality"—to exert all of your psychological energy to burst through initial obstacles until you achieve a free-flowing momentum to achieve your goals.

Think of a rocket ship that exerts a lot of energy to escape from the Earth's gravity, but once it has done so, it needs to expend less energy to keep going. In the same way, you need to escape from your own negative mental gravity—those negative thoughts of fear, regret, and sadness. To do so, you need to expend all of the energy you have at the moment to get beyond that point of resistance.

Once you've done that, you will be much lighter and capable of going much further with less energy and force. In essence, you become self-propelled. Your future successes will create Invincibility Imprints—positive thoughts and habits that give you the motivation, drive, and energy to go even further in your self-transformation. When you get past the mental gravity of your old self-critical thoughts and emotions, you will create a self-perpetuating cycle of excellence and accomplishment. You will be able to blast off into the new space of your transformed self as you reach new heights of self-development and self-mastery.

Here are a few strategies to help you create the Blast Off Mentality:

■ *Do Micro-Tasks*: Aim to do things more efficiently by applying short bursts of energy to your daily tasks; whether it's paying bills, handling email, or shopping. For example, divide tasks into bite-sized or smaller tasks (micro-tasks) that you can do in a shorter period of time. If you hate doing paperwork, give yourself 15 minutes on a particular day to handle some papers. In this short time slot, you may have just enough time to organize the materials and get them ready for more processing. In this way, the mere starting of the task will give you momentum to do more next time.

■ *Focus your energy on the most important thing; don't dissipate your energy*. Avoid wasting your energy and time on low significance activities such as watching TV excessively or randomly surfing the net. Focus instead on the most important purpose you have, whether it is your relationships, mental and physical health, or career/business goals. Pick one thing you want to accomplish each day and place all of your attention on meeting your goal. When you have an undivided mind and heart, you can harness great power for whatever you want to do.

■ *When you're in the flow, keep at it*. There will be times when you will be in a state of flow; a relaxed and enjoyable state of mind in which you are completely absorbed in the task at hand. In this flow state, you lose your self-consciousness and concern about time. You become completely immersed in what you are doing; you and the activity become one. Strive to stay in this flowing mindset for as long as you can. Find a place where you can work, or do your activity, without interruption. Turn off your cell phone and devices—resist the temptation to check your email or texts.

When you are able to create a Blast Off Mentality, you will be able to accomplish much more in a shorter period of time. Aim to maintain this high level of momentum as long as you possibly can, and you will achieve maximum results.

Master the Art of Completion

Now that you have learned how to generate initial momentum to accomplish your goals, your next step is to finish what you start.

Many times, we get in the habit of leaving things unfinished. As a result, our subconscious mind creates a pattern of thinking that we will not complete things. In this way, our mind reinforces our half-hearted attempts to finish tasks, and we may give up when we are getting close to completion and fruition.

The solution lies in one very simple discipline: Finish what you start. Go home and finish that important task you started weeks, months, or even years ago. Complete one important task that you have been putting off, such as calling someone, sending an email, or finishing an important project.

Perhaps, you have been afraid of the consequences of the task, or you have been concerned about your ability to complete it, or to do it well. The reason you didn't do it doesn't matter. What does matter is that you are now willing to take the extra step to internalize the "finish" mentality—making it a part of your automatic mental mechanism: "I finish what I start."

With this finish mentality, you're telling your subconscious mind that if something is worth starting, then it is worth finishing. Consequently, as you complete important tasks, you will have more mental discipline to complete future projects. In the process, your efficiency and sense of satisfaction will skyrocket.

Recognize That Action Is Distilled Intent

You may know people who talk a lot, but do little of what they say they will do. They scatter their words quite aimlessly like seeds on shallow ground, never quite translating their words into action. To become a person of Invincibility, whose words become reality, you need to understand a crucial principle:

Action is distilled intent.

In other words, your action or behavior is what matters in the end. It's not what you say you will do, or what you think about doing, it's what you end up doing that counts the most.

Something is distilled when it is reduced to its essential elements. A person may say one million words over the course of a period of time, but they may do little of what they say. To find out their true intent, you need to get down to the essence of what they actually did, which usually boils down to a few words, "I did it, or "I didn't do it."

Let this sink in for a bit. You may intend, or want to do something. You say, "I intend to lose weight, quit smoking, go back to school, or complete a creative project." To intend is the same as saying the word, "Try." Throughout our lives, we intend, try, or think about trying many things. However, what we actually do is the purified part of that intent; its essence boiled down into a few words.

Either: "I did what I said," or "I didn't do what I said."

Either: "I quit the bad habit," or "I didn't quit the bad habit."

Either: "I achieved my goals," or "I didn't achieve my goals."

A lot of the time, the person who talks a lot doesn't follow through with actions based on their earlier words. Instead of excellence and accomplishment, they have excuses for why they didn't do something. Instead of results, they have reasons for why they didn't complete the task.

A teacher asks the student a simple question, "Did you do the homework?" Either the student says "Yes," and turns it in, or they have a multitude of excuses for not doing it, "My dog ate the homework." "The wind blew it away," "I overslept," and so on. In the end, only the student's action, or inaction, is a strong indicator of their intention to do the homework.

Of course, sometimes life can interfere and create actual emergencies and unforeseen circumstances that prevent someone from accomplishing their intent. But here, we are not talking about exceptions. The majority of the time, it's not unexpected circumstances that block someone from accomplishing what they intended to do; it's their own self-defeating thought process that prevents them from achieving what they set out to do (and which they had the capacity to do).

Think about this concept the next time you hear people promising things to you. Only through their actions do their words have meaning. One person says thousands of words, but only acts on a small portion of them, if any. Another person, an Invincible Mind individual, says fewer words, but acts on nearly all of them. That is the person of true power. The Invincible Mind person focuses on their words as they speak them, so they say what they mean, and they do what they say.

This same principle applies to you. Ask yourself: How many of the words that I express with great fervor do I act on?

Do I really want a great relationship with my ideal partner? Do I really want to get in great shape and have excellent health? Do I really want a career or business that I'm passionate about? Do I really want to create the social life and family life I desire? Do I really want to improve my mind and achieve a state of consistent happiness?

If the answer is truly "Yes," to all of those questions, then you will take concrete and persistent actions to reach those goals. If the answer is "Yes, but (insert an excuse)," or "Maybe," then chances are you didn't have the true intention to complete them in the first place. Or, if you did, something got in your way, and you weren't able to complete the task as originally intended.

You can always find reasons for why you couldn't do something: "I have bad genetics," "People always get in my way," or "I have bad luck." On the other hand, when you take charge of life with your mind of Invincibility, you can always find reasons for why you can do something: "I work extra hard," "I won't take 'no' for an answer," or "God (nature/reality) is on my side."

With a strong self-belief in your ability to do what you say; you will place a great value on keeping your word—whether it is spoken to others or yourself. If you say that you will make a change in your life, or help other people, you will strive to follow-through and take action to make your words come true.

When you live from a mindset of integrity and commitment to your word, you not only have more success in life, but you also feel better about yourself. By translating your words into action, you will have the confidence that you can make good things happen; you are a person who follows through and gets things done.

Promise yourself that, starting today, you will distill your words into a few simple truths, and then act upon them. Tell yourself that you don't have any time to waste with idle words—life is here now; it may not be here tomorrow.

Your distilled words may be something like:

I will achieve my potential and actualize my talents (Don).

I will make a lasting impact on the world.

I will love with all of my heart.

I will create financial security for myself and my loved ones.

I will be healthy and practice self-care.

I will be the best parent, spouse, or friend that I can possibly be.

I will leave a lasting legacy of goodness and love.

By taking action today on the essential words of your soul's desires, you are building your inner and outer power. You are moving toward that promised land of Invincibility: a marvelous place where your dreams come true, and your love and passion can be shared joyfully with others.

Your Invincibility Blueprint is Ready

To create your personal Invincibility Blueprint—your guide to sustained excellence—you need to instill positive ingrained patterns and habits in yourself. You do this by taking small but decisive actions, day by day, until you establish a mental pathway to success. Instead of contracting your mindset, you will expand it as you surpass problems and obstacles to achieve your most treasured goals.

In the end, your intention will become reality, and you will grow yourself into the person you've always wanted to be.

Chapter Fifteen

Create Unstoppable Relationships

Would you like to have unstoppable relationships? Relationships that are loving, harmonious, productive, and lasting? If the answer is "Yes," then it's important for you to associate yourself with the best people you can find for your friendships, business associations, and romantic relationships.

We start by examining the world of people, and see that there are two main types of individuals in the psychological sense: Invincibility Seekers and Negativity Seekers.

Invincibility Seekers are those individuals who strive to be the best they can possibly be. They focus on mastering their inner states of being and creating thoughts of compassion, empathy, love, creativity, and confidence to elevate themselves and others. They have emotional intelligence and are psychologically mature. They exude kindness, goodness, decency, love, and strength. These Invincibility Seekers can contribute greatly to your growth and happiness in life.

Negativity Seekers, on the other hand, are those individuals who reside at a low psychological level of development. They are critical, selfish, complaining, negative, and aggressive. In the beginning, they can seem to be your best friend or ideal romantic partner. But, then at some point, they revert back to their true nature: a negative and emotionally draining person who can suck the life out of you. If you let them, they can make your existence a living hell.

When we classify people into Invincibility Seekers or Negativity Seekers, we are not looking at superficial traits or surface differences. We are not evaluating people based on looks, connections, intelligence, and educational attainment; or financial, career, and social status. There are Negativity Seekers from among the rich and the poor; there are Invincibility Seekers from all walks of life.

What does matter is the person's level of emotional maturity and psychological development as a good, kind, and decent human being. Does the person exude compassion, patience, confidence, and goodwill to others?

At this point, you may be thinking: What about everyone else in the middle? Those who are neither Invincibility Seekers nor Negativity Seekers. How do we understand those individuals?

Those in the middle can be seen as Status Quo People—they are settled into their present life, and may even be comfortable to a degree, although they may not be entirely happy or successful. They have found a certain level of psychological comfort or security—some more than others—and are living their lives as best they can. However, since they are not focused on their inner development, they often suffer when their Self-Defeating Mind kicks in and invades them with thoughts of anger, sadness, fear, regret, and deprivation.

The other danger for Status Quo People is that they are vulnerable to being infected by the negativity of a world that is dominated by Negativity Seekers. They can become victims of mood contagion and pick up the negative energies of other people. Mood contagion occurs when other people infect you with their negative moods, and you start to feel like they're feeling: frustrated, fearful, angry, and unhappy. If you're a Status Quo person, you may not have constructed the emotional shield you need to protect yourself from the negative people of the world; as a result, you suffer from their downward energies.

Although some Status Quo people may have a relatively pleasant life, they can enjoy much more happiness and success if they become Invincibility Seekers. Notice that the term "Seeker" is used here—a person who is striving to become better and grow as a human being. As an Invincibility Seeker, you are seeking excellence in your inner and outer life, and you want to help those around you reach the same state.

Being an Invincibility Seeker, however, doesn't mean that you are perfect. It just means that you have made the decision to work on yourself and become the best person you can possibly be: morally, psychologically, physically, emotionally, and spiritually. It means that you want to help other people and make a positive impact on the world.

How to Recognize Invincibility Seekers: Your Best Friends in the World

When you're out in the social or work world, it's important that you learn how to recognize Invincibility Seekers so you can form a positive connection with them.

How do you recognize a true Invincibility Seeker?

First, you will see that they are full of energy; people feel better and more comfortable around them. Invincibility Seekers extend their compassion to others; they are kind, loving, forgiving, and patient. Also, they are natural, authentic, and confident without having to brag or boast. They have stopped trying to impress others with a façade because they know that the best way to live is to be true to themselves and others.

Here are some of the characteristics of an Invincibility Seeker you should be on the lookout for when choosing your friends and life partner:

- **They are in tune with the rhythms of life**. Normally, they are patient people who take their time doing what they need to do, with full awareness. At the same time, they recognize that they may need to act quickly and decisively when there is an emergency or urgent matter at hand. Overall, they are flexible and can adapt well to the needs of any situation.

- **They're secure within themselves.** They don't place unwanted pressure on you to do what you don't want to do. They are so inwardly balanced in their mindset that they don't need to argue with you about the best way to act in life. They lead by their noble example, more than just mere words.

- **They're the peacemakers of society.** When other people are creating conflict for its own sake, and wallowing in the negative excitement of hostility, they rise above the fiery mess with their peace and poise. Their mere presence helps bring an end to conflict and fosters harmony where there is discord.

Although Invincibility Seekers are the type of people you want to spend the most time with, you will undoubtedly run across Negativity Seekers—negative, critical, and weak-minded people who try to drag you down to their level. Because of their ability to cause pain and destruction in your life, it's important to study the Negativity Seeker nature carefully and be able to identify them when they are around you.

How to See Through Negativity Seekers

Negativity Seekers are everywhere—they can be in your home, workplace, or neighborhood—their gloom, doom, and critical natures permeate everywhere they go. Although they can make other people suffer, they often suffer just as much from their own self-defeating thoughts and actions.

You may be wondering: Why would anyone be a Negativity Seeker and intentionally suffer from thoughts of anger, conflict, depression, and regret? The answer is that Negativity Seekers often don't see themselves as negativity seekers. They see themselves as being right or suffering from the actions of others. They usually don't realize that much of their negative mindset is self-created; they do much of the damage to themselves by thinking in gloomy and self-defeating ways.

In a certain sense, Negativity Seekers may even be addicted to negativity because it provides them with a sense of comfort, entitlement, and even excitement—something is always going on in their minds, 24/7: thoughts of gloom and doom, persecution, fear, and anger. Their heads are so full of negativity, it's like they're having one big "Negativity Party" surrounded by dozens of partygoers who bring their own negativities to the event: fear, doubt, sadness, anger, regret, and so on.

Here are some characteristics of a Negativity Seeker:

- **They spread their negativity everywhere.** Like a virus, they love to spread anger, fear, regret, and sadness everywhere they go.

- **They think they are better than other people.** They have a strong sense of entitlement and false superiority, thinking they are better than everyone else. They often delight in arguing how they are right and you are wrong. They like making you feel inferior so they can feel better about themselves.

- **They love to gossip and criticize.** They like to talk about other people's flaws because it gives them a sense of excitement and empowerment—a feeling of being alive. When others make a mistake, they are quick to pounce on them and disparage their reputation. They are excellent mockers—making fun of people is their favorite pastime.

- **They live in misery.** Although they would probably deny it, they live in a miserable state of mind. Rarely happy for long, they suffer from their own negative natures; they are punished by their own personalities. They are like a rabid, aggressive dog that is set loose to attack others. What they don't know is that the same anger and aggression they direct outwardly will come back to bite them as well.

- **They rarely want to change.** They may tell you how much they are open to improving themselves, but in reality, they usually aren't. They are content to stay in their negativity prison, and may even become angry at you if you try to help them escape. They say, "How dare you tell me how to live. I know the way."

At first glance, you can be fooled by Negativity Seekers because some of them may appear to be quite bright, attractive, and charming. They smile, they laugh, they complement you. But, under their masks, they are petty and calculating individuals who are ready to pounce on you at the slightest appearance of weakness.

> *Simon, an outside sales rep in his mid-30s, was as charming as charming could be. His infectious smile and laugh lit up any room he walked into, and his 6'4" muscular frame made an impressive entrance. He also fancied himself as quite the ladies' man. After captivating a woman's heart, he would date her for a few weeks—soaking up her affection and attention. Then, he would discard her like a worn out pair of shoes; leaving behind a trail of broken promises and hurt feelings. In his distorted mind, he thought he was doing the women a favor: He couldn't help it if the ladies loved him. That was their fault for getting too emotionally involved. He was just having fun.*

True Negativity Seekers are skilled at wearing masks of happiness or satisfaction. There are several variations of these masks. There is the smiling mask. The wise mask. The excited mask. The loving mask. The benevolent mask. However, if you were to look underneath the masks, you would see their arrogance, deceit, manipulation, and anger—the ugly personality they possess inside.

As you look to distinguish between Negativity Seekers and Invincibility Seekers, you may wonder: "How do I determine the kindness of a person?"

Simple—by seeing how they act when they don't need you anymore. Anyone can be kind to someone they need something from, whether it is practical advantages, money, sex, affection, approval, or psychological benefits. But, once those advantages and benefits are no longer there, how does the person treat you? Are they loving or cold? Are they kind or cruel?

The Negativity Seeker will act in a cold and unkind manner when they can no longer obtain an advantage over you, while an Invincibility Seeker will maintain calmness of mind regardless of what they receive, or don't receive, from you.

Many times, a person's kindness vanishes as soon as the benefits and advantages go away from being with a person. Then, their mask comes off, and this "kind" person bares their teeth. Now you see the Negativity Seeker for what they really are, and always were: an angry, deceitful, and self-centered individual who doesn't really care about you as a human being; they were only interested in what they could get from you.

In the beginning, after you do a favor for a Negativity Seeker, they may appear to overflow with gratitude, with a profuse, "Thank you so much." The next time you do them a favor, there will be a curt, "Thank you." The third time they will angrily demand why you didn't help them sooner.

If this happens to you, don't despair. This is actually the greatest news you can have because you finally see the person for who they really are—a Negativity Seeker who wishes to harm you, or take advantage of you.

You may have caught glimpses of their Negativity Seeking behavior earlier in the relationship—the rudeness to servers and others; the pettiness, selfishness, critical nature, and lack of self-control. Yet, chances are, you were blinded by their charisma, looks, pleasing personality, or the benefits they were promising you.

The good news is that the more of an Invincibility Seeker you become—the further you go on your self-development journey—the easier it will be for you to distinguish between Negativity Seekers and Invincibility Seekers. You will be able to see behind the Negativity Seekers' masks before they take them off.

As a result, you will save yourself a lot of heartache, suffering, and disappointment. You will immediately recognize Negativity Seekers for who they are: Weak actors who try to hide behind a mask of goodwill, when in reality, they have little inside except resentment, anger, selfishness, and negativity.

When you recognize a Negativity Seeker for who they really are, you will be able to distance yourself from them. You will protect your inner nature from their attacks, and you will serve as an example to them of what true Invincibility looks like.

Protect Yourself From Negativity Seekers

Once you know how to identify Negativity Seekers, your next step is to learn how to protect yourself from them—especially when you have to be around them. Sometimes, you can't avoid Negativity Seekers. You live with them or work with them; they may be a part of your family, or even a spouse or love partner.

If that is the case, what do you do to prevent them from infecting you with their negativity? You need to separate yourself—your psyche and emotional health—from their influence. You can learn how to put up a psychological force field or shield that protects you from the negative "emotional bullets" fired at you by Negativity Seekers—those who are at a low level of psychological and spiritual development.

Try this exercise:

Exercise: Be the Doctor

Imagine that the Negativity Seeker is a patient in a mental hospital, and you are the doctor. You can offer them medicine (advice), but you can't make them take it. They may refuse to take it (they often don't want it), and may even yell at you for offering it, "How dare you try to change me?"

Although their rantings and ravings may have scared or hurt you in the past, things are different now. You realize the truth: You are the doctor, and they are the patient. As the patient, they are trapped in the mental hospital of their own negativity and anger. As the doctor, you can go home—your peaceful mind—any time you want to.

What a great feeling it is to be able to shed the negativity of the last person you interacted with. When you do this, the Negativity Seeker is separated from your emotional presence, and you are able to live free in your own pleasant mind. If they want to change, you can help them from the comfort of your own mental security because their negativity no longer invades you like it did before.

Negativity Seeker Defense

To further immunize yourself against Negativity Seekers, here are some effective weapons you can use:

1. See Them as Suffering from Themselves. Negativity Seekers are their own punishment. All of us live in our own minds. Our minds can be a palace full of pleasurable and happy thoughts, or it can be a prison full of negativity, complaints, regrets, and insecurities.

When someone is criticizing you, or being mean to you, realize that they are also suffering from the fiery force of their own words. When they attack you, watch as their face becomes red, they clench their fists, and they tremble in anger. Their blood pressure goes up, and their mind is a whirlwind of aggression and pain.

The reality is that they are harming themselves, physically and psychologically, with the very negativity they are trying to force on you.

Instead of fearing them, or being angry at them, simply maintain a calm and compassionate state. Closely observe how much they suffer from their own Self-Defeating personality. See them as weak and helpless human beings who have nothing to do with the real Invincible You.

Think of the Negativity Seeker like a lion who is caged in a zoo. When you visit the zoo, you can look at the lion behind the cage, but you don't need to fear it because it is trapped behind the cage—it can do nothing to harm you. The lion can roar all it wants, but its fierce roar cannot hurt you.

In the same way, Negativity Seekers are trapped behind the cage of their own negativity. You may have compassion for them, but you also recognize how dangerous they are if you get too close to them. Call out advice to them if you like, but keep a safe distance so they won't bite your head off.

2. Refuse Their "Gift of Negativity." Negativity is not really a gift; it is actually a booby trap primed to explode at a moment's notice.

However, the person giving the negativity thinks it's a gift because that is all they have to give.

Your best approach when dealing with a Negativity Seeker is to refuse to accept that person's negativity. When someone gives you a gift in real life, and you politely refuse it, where does the gift go? To the original gift-giver, of course. If you don't want it, you can simply return it to the person who gave it to you.

Here's what you can do if someone wants you to gossip about a friend. You can simply refuse the "gift of gossip" and say to yourself (or to the gossiper):

"I don't talk about other people when they're not present. Thanks for offering me a gift of gossip, but I don't desire it. I give it back to you."

Do the same with any other so-called gifts—anger, fear, and sadness— or any other negative emotional states that others try to infect you with. Make sure you return it to the person who tried to give it to you. When Negativity Seekers try to control you with their "Gift of Negativity," you say to them, mentally or verbally: "I will no longer sacrifice my natural integrity to you. I am now living my own life."

You can say this without any hostility, but only with calm assurance. Doing this releases a tremendous amount of power and energy within yourself, and liberates you from the negative emotional contamination of Negativity Seekers.

3. Learn the Reverse Lesson. Here's a lofty thought: Let the negativity in others teach you how to be the opposite way. You can learn the importance of peace from an angry person, patience from an impatient person, and love from an unloving person. Think of everyone in your life as a teacher. Even the most difficult, aggressive, mean-spirited, and hateful person on earth can teach you a Reverse Lesson. The Reverse Lesson is applied when you do the opposite of what a Negativity Seeker does: When you respond to anger with calmness, rudeness with kindness, and impatience with patience.

For example, you can learn the Reverse Lesson—love and acceptance— from a person who is hateful and critical because you observe the steep price the Negativity Seeker pays for their aggressive nature. You see how others secretly resent them. You see how the angry person's face becomes red and how their breath is out of control. You also observe their failed business and personal relationships and the problems they experience because of their negativity and aggression.

You will clearly observe all of the emotional damage done by the angry person—both to themselves and others. As a result, you will resolve to be the opposite: peaceful, loving, and embracing. You will focus on the strengths of others, and you will forgive the flaws and mistakes they make. You will be slow to criticize and quick with praise; you will extend compassion and understanding to others.

With this new "go higher" mindset, you will no longer criticize unkind and troublesome people. In fact, you have compassion for them. You realize that no one can get away with their badness—they are their own punishment.

Instead of being outraged by the Negativity Seeker, thinking, "How could they do that? Why do they hurt me?" you will think to yourself, "I know you suffer from yourself, and I have empathy for your pain, but I don't wish to live like that. I choose to be free."

With this new perspective, you can act kindly to the unkind because you realize they have to live with themselves for the rest of their unhappy lives, unless they truly want to change. The good news is that, by applying the reverse lesson of the angry and condemning person, you have liberated yourself to become more peaceful and loving. You have taken another step toward your own mental elevation.

4. Attract Your Own Level. People often ask this question: Why does an insecure person attract an abusive one? The answer is simple: Because they occupy the same low psychological level of development—only in different forms. The insecure person unconsciously attracts an abuser because that is what feels "natural" to them, while the abuser unconsciously attracts an insecure person because that is what feels "comfortable."

These patterns often begin in childhood. The child victim of abuse or neglect may unconsciously seek more of the same abusive treatment in an adult partner because they expect to be treated like that, mistakenly thinking that is "what they deserve." Or, they can go the other way and become an abusive or manipulative person. They may place their spouse or children in the same position they were in as a child by harming them in psychological or physical ways.

Neither the insecure person nor the abuser is truly natural or comfortable. They are both suffering from their own weakened states of mind. It happens every day: Two Negativity Seekers get together in a relationship and promise each other roses and champagne. Before long, however, their true negative natures reveal themselves, and things can get bad in a hurry.

How about you? Do you keep finding Negativity Seekers to get involved with? If so, remember the following relationship advice: To cease being hurt by others, stop hurting yourself. Your inner criticism of yourself is what opens the door for a Negativity Seeker to come into your life to criticize and hurt you.

Both hurts are part of the same movement—one is internal from your own thoughts; the other is external, coming from someone else. When you love yourself, you will neither attract, nor respond, to the negativity of others.

To attract Invincibility Seekers as friends and romantic partners, you need to work on yourself first. Read, think, meditate, pray, study yourself and others, and associate with Invincibility Seekers—those who are kind, loving, giving, and compassionate. The more Invincible you become, the more you will attract those who share a similar mindset. Once you start to become a happier, more fulfilled, and integrated human being, you will discover a miracle: The old negative "friends" and relationships in your life will fade away, and you will attract more loving, compatible, healthy, and fulfilling human connections.

Say "No" to Negativity Seeker Bullies

Negativity Seekers are more than just criticizers and complainers. They can also be terrible bullies who intrude, push, and harass their way into your personal space and deeply held values—trying to impose their will and forcing you to do things you don't want to do. If you've encountered a bullying Negativity Seeker, you need to learn about a great power that exists within you. It consists of one simple word, "No."

Although it may seem difficult to say, especially to people who hold some type of influence over you, "No," has the power to bring tremendous positive change into your life and the lives of others.

When pushy, argumentative, aggressive, and intimidating people try to control you, just say "No," inwardly or outwardly. Sternly refuse to let anyone put pressure on you to do what you don't want to do, whether it's to give them money, attention, sex, approval, material advantages, or to agree with them.

When they try to pressure you, just be calm, but firm. Say to them, either verbally or internally: "No. I will not do it. Knock it off."

The emotional bully will probably resent it when you say this; you have just called their bluff. But, there will also be a part of them, a secret inner part, that is glad you didn't bend to their childish pressure. Some of them may even secretly admire that you stood up to them. Perhaps, they will never say it to you, but it's part of their thought process.

Part of their mind may even wish that they didn't have to be bullies— that they could earn respect and admiration from others by living with confidence instead of intimidation. Yet, most of the time, they remain bullies because that is all they know how to be.

Regardless of the bully's real or perceived reaction, it makes no difference to you. You will say "No," and you will stick to your true desires. You will always have your "No" handy at your disposal—you will refuse to do things that are not right for you.

Unfortunately, the real world is full of tactless and overbearing people who will try to bully you. Realize that you have the power to stand your ground and refuse to consent to a relationship based on fear. When you say "No," the relationship won't necessarily be ended immediately, but you will end the fear behind it. Eventually, the relationship will transform itself naturally—one of you may leave it, or the other person may decide to change.

Although the bully may threaten you with loss and pain, their primary power over you is usually the power you give them—by your fear and self-doubt. When you fear a bully, their bullying often grows because they thrive on your fearfulness.

To diminish the fear you have toward an intimidating bully, picture them as a small baby who is still in diapers. They are crying and howling for milk and attention, and they are really helpless unless someone gives them what they clamor for. You are the adult; you can simply say, "No, I'm not having that." Put the tantrum-throwing bully in "time-out" mentally and remove them from your inner life. You are the one in charge here, not them. Use "No" as your tool of discipline and training to deal with immature minds who act out in foolishness and anger.

Think about it: By using the power of "No," you have a secret weapon to combat difficult and draining people. The extra benefit is that by saying "No" to the things you don't want, you are automatically saying "Yes" to all the things you *do* want.

You are saying "Yes" to love, authenticity, and right connection.

You are saying "Yes" to following your dreams and goals and helping other like-minded people achieve their objectives.

Invincibility Seeker Relationships: The Greatest Love of All

Invincibility Seeker relationships are the best in the world. Invincibility Seekers are positive, helpful, supportive, and loving people. Ideally, you would have as many Invincibility Seeker friends as possible, and you would have a lasting love relationship with an Invincibility Seeker as well.

The greatest romantic love of all is Invincibility Seeker love—when two people help each other improve their lives and bring light into the world. This is a beautiful relationship of likeminded "soul-enhancers" who are helping to enhance each other's souls to reach a level of living that is far beyond the ordinary.

When you think about having a relationship with an Invincibility Seeker partner, realize that meeting one is much different than finding a typical love partner. You don't need to chase, pursue, or convince them to love you. You don't have to "win them over," or "capture their heart." The beauty of it is that you just simply need to raise your own Invincibility level. This means that you will love yourself first. To love yourself means that you are true to yourself—you go for what you actually want in life; you express the way you really feel.

In the real world, people are emotionally drained by inauthenticity. This is especially true in the world of dating and romance. A person wants to find someone to love, but meets endless frustrations in their quest. To impress a dating candidate, many singles wear a psychological mask that hides their true nature. Then, when the masks come off, they are often disappointed to discover that they were not nearly as compatible as they originally thought.

When an Invincibility Seeker meets a Negativity Seeker, the Invincibility Seeker will quickly realize that they have nothing in common. Although they may have a surface attraction, it would be impossible for them to have a lasting and loving relationship because they are residing in widely separated psychological levels. There is no real attraction because like attracts like.

While it is true that certain differences in a couple can be attractive, and even complementary, most successful long-term relationships are based on compatibility (or similarity) at the deepest level of values, beliefs, and goals. This is especially true when evaluating psychological or spiritual compatibility—two people who are similar in their levels of inner development and desire to grow their Invincibility together. If a person wants to attract an Invincibility Seeker mate, they need to become an Invincibility Seeker themselves—developing the qualities of compassion, gentleness, kindness, empathy, and patience.

True love in romantic relationships blossoms when two people fully and deeply understand each other—when they have a sincere desire to share a higher psychological and spiritual life together. Their mutual affection grows as they awaken to their true natures. When two people are their true and authentic selves, they will be united in love. They can't hurt each other because pure understanding passes back and forth between them. They may be different physically, or in their personalities, but both are individual reflections of the single Supreme (God or nature), which consists of pure love.

At a higher level, love becomes a quiet consideration and empathetic understanding of another person. When one partner finds their lover's prized item which has been lost for days, and quietly places it on the dresser, that is love. When a husband has his wife's bubble bath ready for her because he knows she had a hard day at work (or home), that is love.

The other important thing to recognize about an Invincibility Seeker relationship is that they are not based solely on surface characteristics like looks or charm. Many times, people put others on a pedestal just because they are attractive, intelligent, or successful. When they do this, they are engaging in a form of false worship.

It's important to realize that others are not better than you. You, too, have special qualities that are attractive and appealing. And, the most attractive quality of all is your Invincibility: Your authenticity, creativity, patience, compassion, and love.

When you meet the right Invincibility Seeker partner, you will have a love like no other—one that is not just based on meeting each other's surface needs such as sex or companionship. Instead, it is founded on a pure and deep understanding of the other—knowing each other's goals, habits, dreams, preferences, values, fears, and hopes. This leads to a total acceptance of the beloved as they are—forming the foundation of a powerful and lasting love that doesn't fade when the looks or status goes away. It will be a love affair that stands the test of time and is based on giving love without expectation—the greatest love of all.

Sexual Transmutation: Your Energy Source for Maximum Triumph

When aiming to create unstoppable relationships, it's important to understand the power of sexual energy. Sex can be a powerful force for both creativity and destruction. Unfortunately, too many people misuse their sexual power and waste it in momentary exchanges of lust, power, and pleasure.

There is a higher purpose for your sexuality that can help you reach your Invincible Mind. It is known as Sexual Transmutation. Sexual transmutation, also known as Brahmacharya in the East (Bhagwan, 2016), and sublimation in the West, is the utilization of sexual energy for creative, humanitarian, and spiritual purposes—it's the investment of sexual energy in a person, activity, or idea for a higher purpose.

The instinctual sexual drive is one of the most powerful forces and motivations for human beings. More than simply the need to procreate and pass along our genes, sexuality represents the need for excitement, pleasure, power and submission, intimacy, ecstasy, and love, as well as deep, meaningful connection. But, at the same time, when sexuality is untamed and unchanneled, it can be a distraction and a negatively disruptive force for both individuals and society.

Sexual transmutation is the ideal use of sexuality. It is the channeling of human sexual energy into a higher state or frequency that can contribute positively to the individual and society. To achieve sexual transmutation, you need to stimulate your mind to operate at a higher than average plane by using a mental stimulant that combines some of the most powerful forces on earth: sex, love, and romance.

In our daily lives, we may get good ideas, but they often slip by—our minds are often distracted and don't have the capacity to hold higher awareness. We don't retain our higher ideas because our minds are distracted by the needs and desires of everyday life—especially the desire for romantic/sexual attraction and expression. Consequently, if we indulge in actual sexual activity to excess, our mind can lose its strength.

A healthier approach would be to transmute your sexual energy from pure physical desire to a higher desire to help, create, and contribute to humanity. When you do this, you are able to raise your mental state to a much higher frequency of energy, and you can accomplish much more in the process.

With sexual transmutation, you don't deny or repress your sexual urges; instead, you consciously channel or focus them on a higher or noble cause. People of higher intellect and spiritual goodness are able to stimulate their minds to vibrate at a superior level by using their sexual energy in an intelligent way.

Apply Sexual Transmutation to Your Daily Life

There are two ways to practice sexual transmutation.

One is to invest your libido, or sexual energy, in a loved partner who is also loving to you. Both of you extend loving energy without expectation toward each other. In this way, your sexual energy becomes fused with love and romance, and inspires both of you to achieve the greatest heights of success and love in your personal relationships and lives. Sex is the excitable and passionate element, while love is the calming emotional substance that enhances your purpose, poise, accuracy of judgment, and balance. This love-sex-romance combination is truly the ultimate chemistry of the mind that can change everything.

The second approach to sexual transmutation is to maintain celibacy or minimal sexual activity, and instead use your sexual and love energy to accomplish great things in the world. These may include inventions, works of art, and literary pieces as well as business and humanitarian ventures. Or, you may apply your energy by being fully present as a loving parent, friend, and work associate.

It's true that you are a more attractive and charismatic person when you transmute (or channel) your sex energy, instead of spending it excessively on nonproductive sexual physical activity. This is especially the case if you add love into the mix—the love you express to humanity, as well as to your loved partner.

When you combine sex and love in this way, and create a fantastic love mixture, your whole persona and nature will change. Your handshake will be warmer, your posture is straighter, and your voice is more melodious. You have infused your body and mind with an unstoppable elixir that encourages creative, loving, and healthy thoughts while discouraging the presence of destructive emotions.

Think of Sexual Transmutation as a way to "turn up" the vibrations of sexuality into a form of intelligence, even genius. Many people lower themselves below animals when they misuse the great sexual force that has been given to them. Even animals indulge their sex natures in moderation. A majority of animals have sex only in certain seasons; thereby harmonizing with the laws of nature. Humans, on the other hand, have an "open sexual season" in which they may waste their powerful sexual energy on physical motions that have limited meaning or significance.

The important part of Sexual Transmutation is to encourage the presence of sex, love, and romance as dominating thoughts in your mind that are uplifted for creative and humanitarian purposes. The emotion of love needs to be added to sexual energy because, with love, humans enhance their artistic and aesthetic natures. Love leaves a mark on the soul even after the fire of sexual passion has subsided. Memories of love never pass; they linger long after the source of stimulation has faded.

We have seen people who have been stimulated to great heights of achievement by love, especially by what is known as "agape," or unconditional love. When you love deeply, you commune with an infinite intelligence. As you blend love, sex, and romance, the barrier between the finite mind of man and infinite intelligence is removed. This noble vibration lifts you higher in mind, heart, and soul.

In our society, men and women who have a high sexual energy are often looked down upon with suspicion. They may even be cursed and labeled as defective in some way. As a result, they can develop an inferiority complex and may misuse or dissipate their sexuality in disorganized ways such as random love affairs and loveless sexual liaisons. Or, they repress it and pretend not to be as sexual as they really are. They become overly rigid and sexually repressed people who condemn others for the same sexuality which pulsates inside them.

The reality is that people with a high level of sexual energy can be great leaders, creators, and humanitarians if they learn how to blend their sexual energy with love and romance in the pursuit of a higher and noble purpose, such as helping humanity and spreading love and goodwill. Those individuals who properly channel their sexual energy can become charismatic figures with firm handshakes, attractive tones of voices, and powerful and uplifting vibrations of thought.

In addition, they have more energy, motivation, and perseverance to accomplish their goals because they are driven by the inspiration provided by the lover of their choice. Many battles have been won— many great inventions, businesses, and works of art have been created—when the parties have been motivated by love, sex, and romance.

Here are some examples of love-sex motivation that have led to great accomplishments:

Shah Jahan: Shah Jahan built the Taj Mahal, one of the New Seven Wonders of the World, in memory of his wife. It took 22 years to build with experts gathered from all around the world to help build it.

F. Scott Fitzgerald and Zelda Fitzgerald: Esteemed author, F. Scott Fitzgerald, and his wife, Zelda Fitzgerald, were considered the most famous couple from the Golden Age of Jazz in the 1920's. The writer loved her very much and refused to leave her when she was diagnosed with schizophrenia. F. Scott Fitzgerald tried everything he could to help her and made her the inspiration for the female protagonists of his novels.

Kass and Michael Lazerow: This married couple founded Buddy Media, a social enterprise software company connecting top advertising firms with consumers. In his article, "Why I Have Sex With My Co-founder," Michael makes the case for couples to start businesses together. He explains: "Working with my wife is easy, far easier than working with someone I barely know. Our skill sets are perfect complements."

Bill and Melinda Gates: One of the wealthiest technology innovators in the world, Bill Gates, and his wife, Melinda, are well known for creating The Bill and Melinda Gates Foundation—working to improve the lives and health of people in developing countries, and in the United States.

Casey Sackett and Jennifer Wong: When husband and wife, Casey Sackett and Jennifer Wong, were expecting their first child, Jennifer wanted to find a better way to track, capture, and share her pregnancy journey. As a result, she and her husband created various apps for expectant mothers, including the popular BabyBump, a pregnancy and social network app.

Throughout history, there are numerous examples of great accomplishments that were fueled by passion and love for a romantic partner or spouse. Working together, and inspiring each other through their sexual and love union, these couples were able to accomplish great things for themselves and humanity.

Again, the key to Sexual Transmutation is to fuse sexuality with love. Since sex can be an uncontrollable force, love, and its cousin, romance, is the emotion that serves as a safety valve—giving you calmness, confidence, peacefulness, and harmony. This combination can drive you to heights of super achievement and happiness.

When you transmute your sexual energy, and combine it with love and romance, you will have the right chemistry of mind to achieve your greatest goals. You will be able to obtain ideal health, maximize your potential, and love deeper and better than ever before.

Chapter Sixteen

Wealth Without Limits

Would you like to be rich beyond your wildest dreams? For some people, getting rich, or at least financially comfortable, is one of their primary goals in life. While there are great nonmonetary riches such as love, family, friendship, contribution, creativity, and spirituality, there are also monetary riches which include material possessions, luxury experiences, and cold hard cash.

Having financial wealth can be a blessing for those who receive it because it can give them a sense of financial security and the freedom to pursue the things they truly desire: travel, fun family and social times, new experiences and adventures, sensory pleasures, and compassionate helping of the needy.

Most of all, financial wealth can give us what is perhaps the most valuable asset of all: time. The time to do what we truly desire instead of being hampered by the constraints of a job or a career that takes up too much of our time and energy, and prevents us from doing what we really want to do.

Although the right use of money can produce positive outcomes, the truth is that many people have hang-ups about money. Some avoid it, thinking they will be tainted by a superficial and materialistic focus. Others greedily pursue money and make it the primary focus of their existence. A large number of people have fear towards it. They wallow in the anxiety that they don't have enough money, and will never have enough, to meet their needs and desires.

Money as Loving Energy (LME)

There is a superior way to look at material wealth: Think of Money as Loving Energy—as a positive energy force that travels between human beings to enhance the lives of those it touches, and to make the world a better place.

Loving money energy (LME) works like this: When you do something you love for work (hopefully that is the case), you receive money in the form of loving energy in appreciation for the work you've done. Then, you take that money and purchase goods and services—thereby giving your loving energy in appreciation for the value you receive from another.

On and on, this loving money energy cycle continues as the money and loving energy travels across the world. Money, however, is not just designed for the consumption of material goods. Although material things can bring pleasure and comfort, the key is the use of money as a conscious vehicle for expressing love and improving the lives of others: to heal the sick and empower the powerless, to protect the earth's resources, to reduce crime, violence, and poverty, and to build happy and productive societies.

In this new way of thinking, money is not just a vehicle of exchange for goods and services. It is a powerful force for good that can enhance lives and bring positive emotions into the world. It is a channel for personal growth and harmonious relationships—a way to spread gratitude and positivity throughout the world.

By seeing money as loving energy, you will learn how to speak the language of true wealth and abundance instead of the language of psychological poverty—the fear of scarcity and the frantic belief that you must compete for dwindling resources.

As you delve into the world of loving money energy, you first need to understand the opposing force that can keep you from achieving your full financial potential: The Mind of Scarcity.

The Mind of Scarcity: There's Never Enough

With the Mind of Scarcity, you see money as something you need to hoard and keep to yourself; you think you have to get as much of it as you possibly can so you can live a better life. At the same time, this scarcity mindset makes you anxiously believe that there is not enough money to go around—it convinces you to fight for every dollar.

In your mind, you may say phrases like "Money is tight," and "Money doesn't grow on trees." You worry that you don't have the luck or capacity to make the money you need to make. You fear that other people will try to take your money; you worry that they want to cheat, rob, or take advantage of you.

When you have the Mind of Scarcity, you're afraid that you won't have enough money in life, or that you will lose what little you have. As a result, you are always running around trying to grab more money. You see the money game as a win-lose proposition: One person has to win; the other has to lose.

If you believe there isn't enough money to go around, you will often end up feeling frustrated. You worry that other people, or the world, are conspiring against you to take the money that should be yours. With this mindset you start to retract your energy, and you become tightened and hardened psychologically.

If money scarcity is an issue in your life, then you need to increase your Mind of Abundance.

Mind of Abundance and LME (Loving Money Energy)

The Mind of Abundance is the belief that you will have all the money you need, and that the world will work in your favor to bring you the financial security you desire. When you have the abundance mentality, you are able to boldly start new businesses and engage in new ventures or lifestyle changes because you know, deep down, that you will obtain the resources you need to accomplish your goals.

How do you increase your Mind of Abundance?

Begin by imagining that you have the kind of financial abundance represented by the world's money supply, currently estimated at $94 trillion (Desjardins, 2017). In your mind's eye, visualize that you have so much money that you can afford to give away plenty because you will always have more in store for yourself and your loved ones.

LME (loving money energy) works hand in hand with the Abundance Mentality because when you give money to others as a form of loving energy, you reverse the Mind of Scarcity into the Mind of Abundance. Instead of worrying about whether you have enough money, you have an expansive feeling of abundance—you know you can give to others and still have plenty left over for yourself.

Begin today by giving money to worthy and needy individuals. The amount of money you give doesn't matter. It can be small at first— give some money to the homeless; donate some items to a nonprofit charity; help your neighbor or friend with a small loan or favor. When you give, visualize that you are imparting loving energy to the person or cause. As you do this, you will begin to reverse your mindset of money anxiety and lack, and turn it into one of prosperity and abundance. With this new perspective, you realize that the more loving money energy you give to others, the more it will come back to you.

Although this loving money energy attitude may not be easy to grasp at first, you will begin to notice the positive changes when you apply it to your life. When you change your thinking from money scarcity to money abundance, you will be able to attract more material and spiritual riches.

Let's look at an example of a man who applied loving money energy to create the Mind of Abundance in his business ventures.

Steven, a bus driver and small business owner in his mid-40s, considered himself to be a frugal man. He saved every penny he made and didn't spend much. His father had been a big land speculator and had lost a lot of money. Because Steve didn't want to repeat his father's mistakes, he ended up becoming very tight with his money. At his wife's insistence, however, he began to attend a spiritual center that encouraged abundance thinking—the idea that giving more to others would increase the supply coming back to him.

Skeptical at first, Steven started to try out some of the ideas he had learned, such as putting money out into the community to do good. He invested a small sum in his friend's coffeeshop— the investment paid off, and he made a nice profit (people in the community loved the place). He started giving his time and money to a local charity, and he ended up making some useful business contacts that helped him make even more money.

Eventually, he bought some low-income housing and rented it to some of the formerly homeless people he had helped. Little by little, Steven was starting to see that helping others in a financial way made good sense, not only from a moral ground, but also from a business perspective. He also was feeling good by helping others through his money. He saw how the good he was putting out was coming back to him in many ways, including financially. He was happy that his wife had introduced him to the spiritual place and their interesting ideas.

Give Loving Money Energy Without Expectation

In a practical way, you can enhance your LME by giving away samples of what you love to do for free without expecting anything in return.

If you're a writer, for example, post some of your writing online. If you're a cook, give away one of your favorite homemade dishes to a friend or stranger. If you're a teacher, give a free lesson to a deserving student. When you give what you love to do for free in a conscious and open way, you open up the door for loving money energy to come back to you in the form of real money.

Now you may say, "But, I do that anyway. I sing, teach, act, or paint for free, but I still haven't advanced in my field. I feel like I'm going backward. I'm not appreciated, rewarded, or compensated enough." You may be correct in what you say, but you are missing one important ingredient: To give loving money energy, *without expectation.*

Let's say, for example, that you're an actor. You act in local plays for free; you enjoy the work, but you keep thinking, "When am I going to get my big break? When am I going to make money?"

Although it's important to consider the practical aspects of survival such as food, clothing, and shelter, it's also good to maintain a free-flowing attitude toward loving money energy. Keep perfecting your craft and talent, and give it to the world, without expectation. Don't expect that you have to make a certain amount of money from it, or that you have to be like others who have succeeded in your field. Simply maintain the faith that, if you were meant to be successful with this talent or work, you will receive all the money you need from it.

Farnaz was a single woman in her late-30s who loved to paint since she was a little girl. She had always wanted to be an artist, but her parents discouraged her. They constantly told her to "Find a practical career; otherwise, you will end up broke and miserable."

Heeding her parent's advice, Farnaz started working at a secure government job after college that provided excellent benefits and job security, but she was miserable. She still loved art and would visit galleries on the weekend. After watching a documentary on people who start second careers later in life, she decided to dedicate herself to her art. She bought books and attended art training; she befriended several local artists in her community and began painting. Her specialty was baby paintings—she would paint portraits of the babies of her family and friends—a wonderful remembrance of their infancy.

Initially, she gave away her paintings for free, but as her popularity spread, she started charging for her work. Armed with a self-created website and her homemade YouTube videos, she started publicizing her work and soon appeared on a few podcasts and local TV shows. Her art has become highly sought after, and now she is making a nice living from her work. She left her government job and is having fun doing what she loves the most—creating works of art—while giving joy to parents everywhere.

LME Exercise Number One

If you want to bring more LME (loving money energy) into your life, try this exercise:

Imagine that you are doing what you love, whether it's caretaking, business, writing, teaching, mechanics, science, or the arts. Visualize that you are expressing this activity as a colored light—blue, white, yellow, or green—that is going out to the people you touch through your work. This light represents the loving energy you emanate through your business or career.

Imagine further that this same color light is traveling back to you in the form of actual physical money, whether it's green cash or a blue check. Breathe in, then exhale, as you accept this loving money energy which is returning to you.

As you practice this exercise daily, you will find that you have a different attitude toward work and money. Where before, you may have seen work and money as a way to survive or achieve a sense of security, now you see your work as a conduit to a constant loving money energy transfer—sending out loving money energy and receiving it back. As the loving money energy flows, you will benefit from wonderful experiences and opportunities as you help others do the same.

LME Exercise Number Two: Circulate The $100 Bill of Loving Money Energy

With a group of friends or acquaintances, try this exercise:

Take out a $100 bill and pass it to the person next to you, as you say, "Thank You." Then, that person will pass it along to the person next to them, while saying "Thank You." Each person will take turns giving the $100 bill and saying "Thank You" to the person who received it from them.

Eventually, the $100 bill will come back to you, the original giver of the Loving Money Energy.

This is a fun exercise because you are directly experiencing the power of Loving Money Energy as it travels from person to person and then returns back to the original giver.

As you do this exercise, imagine that when you give someone the $100 bill, you are buying goods and services that were lovingly created by the person who is receiving the money from you. Then, as the Loving Money Energy circulates around the room, each person receiving the money (including you) will visualize that they are working at something they love, and they are receiving the love back in the form of the paper bill known as money.

In this universal exchange of Loving Money Energy, you can experience a tremendous feeling of gratefulness, contribution, and love. On and on, the circle continues as you visualize that Loving Money Energy is spreading throughout the room, your family/community, and the world—bringing joy, comfort, and security to those who those who are touched by LME.

Is Money Your Friend?

As you study the concept of LME, you may wonder why everyone doesn't have the same mindset of prosperity, giving, and growth.

People don't have LME because they lack the right relationship with money. Although they may want more money in their life, a good number of people see money as an enemy instead of a friend. They see money as something they have to fight over; it is always disappearing faster than they can obtain it.

If you have this type of competitive relationship with money, you will forever be frustrated that you don't have enough of money's company. Every time you chase it, it runs away from you. It eludes you and seems to withdraw every time you approach it. The problem is that you are too needy.

It's like when you keep calling a friend who doesn't return your calls. You are begging for their company, but by doing so, you are pushing them further away. It's the same with money. The more you try to force money into your life, the more it will try to elude you.

On the other hand, when you see money as a friend, you act entirely different than before. When you are a friendly person, someone who is likeable, charismatic, and helpful, you will naturally attract friends. Instead of chasing people, they will come to you naturally because they enjoy being with you. They know you have something valuable to offer, whether it's fun, advice, or companionship.

In the same way, treat money as a friend. Develop skills and talents that will attract it. Maybe you're skilled at painting, sales, business, computers, teaching, caretaking, or mechanics. If you're good at something, and it comes naturally to you, focus on perfecting your skill or talent. As we mentioned earlier, you may even give it away for free in the beginning if you want to attract more interest, or you can charge a reasonable fee. The key is to express your talent as much as possible for the benefit of others. If you do that, you will see good things coming to you.

As you share your talent or skills with the world, you will observe that money will come calling as an eager friend. Just as friends come to your place when they know you provide good conversation and delicious food, money will come naturally to you when it realizes that you have something valuable to offer it, and by extension, the world of people.

It's true that money can be one of your best friends when you don't force the relationship and, instead, create the conditions that will attract it.

Do Business to Create Bonds of Cheery Affinity

Another valuable piece of advice deals with buying things or negotiating deals. Your aim in any monetary transaction should be to create "bonds of cheery affinity"—positive feelings resulting in loving business relationships.

Instead of driving the hardest bargain, and squeezing the last dollar out of someone, leave some money on the table. At times, pay a little extra for what you want—not because you are weak or a poor bargainer—but because you want to create a long-lasting and positive relationship with your business associate, vendor, or customer that will last beyond the short time of the present transaction.

Too often, a merchant will try to make the most from their customer, or the customer will try to get the absolute largest financial advantage. Although this is customarily seen as "good business," this type of "win-lose" transactional approach can push potential business partners and customers away because of the lack of harmony and negative feelings sometimes generated by those transactions.

This is especially the case if you, or the person you're dealing with, is a "Feeler" personality—someone who makes decisions primarily based on feelings, emotions, and personal values. You or the other party may take it personally, and even be hurt, by the selfishness and crudeness of people who value money over people.

Since approximately 50% of the population are classified as Feelers (*The Myers & Briggs Foundation*, 2018), it's important to recognize the relational aspects of money. Even if you're a Thinker, and make decisions based on impersonal logic and analysis, it would still behoove you to consider the relational aspects of any business or personal relationship, and to consider "loving energy" as the third party in any business transaction.

In this context, we are not talking about "love" as simply an emotion or romantic/sentimental feeling. With loving money energy, we are discussing a scenario of peace, goodwill, and harmony—a compassionate understanding of the person you are doing business with.

For example, when you slightly overpay a merchant, visualize that you are helping them pay for their child's college education, or for their sick parent's medical bills. You are bringing something positive and loving into their world. And, chances are, they may reciprocate at some point by giving you the better part of the next deal.

Yet, even if they don't return the favor, there will be other business people who will respond to your good gestures, and who will give you more business and better deals as a result of your initial generosity and persona of loving collaboration.

What happens if you do the opposite? If you drive the hardest bargain and aim to squeeze the last penny out of a business deal or transaction? In this case, you have interrupted the loving money energy flow, and you have created a tightened and scarcity-minded relationship. You may think you are doing good business—getting the best value for your money or time—but in reality you may be creating adverse business relationships, especially if the other person feels that you have somehow taken advantage of them.

By taking a larger view of business relationships, and adding harmony and loving energy to the transaction, you have lifted the relationship to a higher point of reciprocal benefit and a bond of cheery affinity. This bond will grow and help facilitate even more positive and satisfying business transactions between you and your business colleague.

At this point, you may be thinking: But how about those unscrupulous people who try to take advantage of my niceness and flexibility? Won't they think of me as weak and try to beat me out of every deal; to squeeze every dollar out of me?

Yes, there are people out there like that, some call them "sharks," who will try to seize every advantage, every perceived weakness, and use it against you in a business transaction. They may try to take advantage of you.

Let them try. You have an antidote to their grasping and scheming ways: your Invincible Mind. Your Invincible Mind is unbeatable because it combines the best of all dimensions: softness and strength; thinking and feeling; flexibility and firmness.

In the real world, although you will be caring and giving in your business relationships, you will also maintain firmness and confidence in your business dealings. You will recognize unethical and manipulative people who only want to greedily take advantage of you. You will also know the inherent worth and value of what you have to offer in a business sense, and you will extend loving energy as long as there is a fair and reciprocal exchange.

When you see the wolf inside a merchant or business associate who is trying to take advantage of your goodwill, you will simply move your loving money energy elsewhere to where it will be appreciated.

You won't grumble or complain about the selfish users; instead, you will realize that they are the victims of their own psychological withholding.

Because of their small-minded and petty natures, these users and manipulators eventually will pay the price in failed business deals, broken business relationships, and missed money-making opportunities. When you discover what they are really like, you will be content because you can move away from them and extend your LME where it will yield the most fruit.

> *Richard described himself as a "shark" in business. He loved to get the best of people in any deal, and he approached every negotiation like a war he had to win at all costs. As a result, he made money, but also alienated a lot of people. Some of his business associates even felt that he had cheated or taken advantage of them—promising things he didn't deliver on. As his reputation for manipulation and deceit spread, Richard saw that his deals were drying up—fewer people wanted to work with him. Soon, he had to move out of the area to a place where people didn't know him as well. He had already burned a lot of bridges, and he didn't seem to want to change. Richard was stuck in a misery of his own making.*

Unfortunately, there are quite a few people like Richard in the world— short-sighted individuals who mistakenly think that a quick financial gain outweighs the longevity of an affirming and mutually beneficial business relationship.

Yet, based on results alone, a practical and ethical business person would soon realize the tremendous business advantage they would obtain if they regularly put compassion and generosity into their business dealings. When you give more in a business transaction in a spirit of goodwill and loving energy, you will often receive more from the world in return.

LME: The New Way to Riches

It's very simple: Once you re-engineer your mind to look at money as loving energy, your entire perspective on finances will change.

Where before, you had worry and doubt, now you have confidence and enjoyment. Soon, you will realize that that there is nothing to fear—no scarcity or lack—when you have the LME Mindset. There is a tremendous amount you can accomplish when love becomes the driving force behind the medium of exchange we call money.

You will not only create more goodwill and positivity around you, but you will also have an abundant new number of financial opportunities and successful ventures. Your profitable business relationships will grow and more people will want to do business with you. Those around you will notice your new attitude toward money and generosity, and some will follow your example of giving loving money energy to the world. When others are inspired by your acts of giving and do the same, it's called "Paying it forward." This can be seen when people pay for the coffee or food of the person behind them in line—and subsequently that person does the same for the person behind them. This chain of generosity is infectious as people realize how good they feel when they help others; in time, the goodwill and loving energy will spread far beyond the original giver.

Of course, there will always be people who will not respond to your new LME approach to life. These are the money sufferers who attach their self-image or ego to how much money they have; to how many possessions they can obtain. They will try to squeeze the most out of every dollar, to get the advantage in every financial transaction; they see other human beings as mere instruments for their money acquisition. While saving money and being frugal can be beneficial, individuals who attach their identity and self-esteem to money often pay the price in terms of emotional and psychological pain. They suffer when they don't think they have enough money, or when they fear losing what they already have. Because they operate from a mindset of scarcity instead of abundance, their daily life is a mad frenzy to accumulate more; they rarely have peace of mind and satisfaction for long.

The solution to this money chase frenzy is to foster the Loving Money Energy Mindset within yourself. Extend loving money energy to others and the world, and you will receive much more in return. With your Loving Money Energy Mindset, each day will bring you more riches. You will receive material riches, including money, possessions, and career/business success, as well as psychological wealth—positive experiences, love, harmony, gratitude, and happiness. This will continue until you, and those you love, will overflow with abundance and prosperity. You will wake up one day and realize the beautiful truth:

You are truly rich—from the inside out.

Chapter Seventeen

The Art of Reversal

Have you ever felt frustrated and stuck in life—trying to accomplish things that seemed difficult or even impossible? If so, now there is a powerful tool at your disposal to help you get what you want in life despite the obstacles and challenges you face.

It is called Reversal.

Reversal is doing the opposite of what you've been doing so you can receive the opposite of what you've been getting. It is a counterintuitive way of thinking in which you do the opposite of what is generally expected, so you can achieve the results you want in your relationships, finances, career, and health.

An example of a reversal is when you momentarily stop trying so hard to achieve something, and instead let people or circumstances come to you (You stop calling someone and wait until they call you). Reversal has power because it completely disrupts the flow of the expected, the routine, and the ordinary. When you apply reversal, something novel and fresh enters your life—a new approach, an innovative solution, a counterintuitive way of thinking—that helps you accomplish your goals.

Let's take a look at some effective Reversals that can help you overcome obstacles and mentally stuck patterns to reach your greatest potential.

Make Friends with What You Reject

One effective reversal is to make friends with what you reject in yourself. Maybe, there is a part of yourself that you call "bad" or "weak," yet you can find great strength in this trait as well.

For example, let's say that you have a short attention span—it's hard for you to focus on one thing at a time for extended periods of time. If that's the case, then you can also see this as a benefit. You may have quick energy bursts that you can use to accomplish a multiple number of tasks.

When you're able to recognize the potential disadvantages of each character trait you may have (short attention span), you can also choose to focus on the positives of that trait (acting quickly and handling various tasks). You do this by using your vocabulary to redefine who you are. Instead of calling yourself "attention-deficit," think of yourself as "multi-attentional." Use the power of words in your favor by defining yourself in your own terms—in Invincible terms.

By embracing the things about yourself that you once thought were weaknesses, your life will be different. By making friends with what you formerly rejected, you will be able to turn a negative into a positive; a mental enemy into a psychological ally. In the end, you will be able to transfer the same trait you thought was a weakness into an asset that will help you achieve what you want.

Turn Fear into Faith

Another powerful reversal you can apply in your daily life is to transform fear into faith. Faith is the belief that things will turn out well for you. Fear, on the other hand, is the belief that something bad is going to happen to you; that you will suffer and lose in life. To live Invincibly, you need to change your fear into faith—having the confident mindset that life will work out in your favor, no matter what problems or challenges you may face.

Here's an exercise you can practice to help you accomplish this reversal:

Exercise: Fear into Faith

Let's say there is something you want—a career, relationship, or lifestyle change—but you are afraid that you won't be able to get it. You think: "I'm not good enough." "I don't have the willpower." "There is too much competition." At this point, fear has a strong hold over you, and you may not go for what you want even though you truly desire it.

Now ask yourself this question: "How would I act differently if I had absolute faith in my abilities to get what I want?"

If, for example, you desire a new job or career opportunity, imagine yourself getting it. Visualize what you will look like, what you will feel like, and where you will be when you accomplish the goal you're aiming for.

Although unreasonable fear usually doesn't go away easily, your faith in a brighter future can begin to mute its power. Each time you see your actualized future—living the way you really want to be—you diminish the stranglehold that fear has over you.

When you start to visualize the successful accomplishment of your goals, you will have a renewed sense of desire and motivation. You will have increased persistence and resilience for overcoming obstacles. Your newfound faith will keep your moving toward your dreams until you accomplish them. You will know firsthand the wonderful feeling of transforming fear into faith.

Have a Self-Kindness Day

Another reversal you can do is to treat yourself kindly instead of always pushing yourself to do more. Although there is nothing wrong with being a high-achieving and hard-working person, some people take it too far and neglect their self-care. As a result, they become less efficient and happy, and may even be vulnerable to mental and physical ailments. To counteract the tendency to work too hard, or care too much for others at the cost of your own mental and physical well-being, be sure to periodically have a Self-Kindness day.

During this special day, you will treat yourself differently. You will savor your accomplishments at the end of the day instead of worrying about all the things you still have to do.

You will also practice self-care: Get enough sleep and eat healthy; indulge in a massage, facial, or getaway to nature; take time to relax and meditate; have fun with friends. Spend time on an exercise program or spiritual practice; partake in a creative hobby. Forgive yourself for any errors you may have made.

Even though self-kindness is a crucial part of your emotional well-being, it's not always easy to practice. You may have the nagging thought that "I don't deserve it; I have to work harder; I have to prove my worth." To transform your thinking, start by realizing that your worth is already established by being a child of creation—you were brought into this earth for a wonderful purpose—to bring light, joy, and contribution to the world. There is nothing you need to do to merit love and kindness. You are already a Queen or King by birthright. Now treat yourself like the inner royalty that you are.

When you treat yourself with kindness, you will not only feel better, but you will also accomplish more because you have additional energy and motivation—the old Self-Defeating thoughts that used to hold you back will begin to vanish. At the same time, people will see the difference in you; as you become more loving to yourself, you will also be more loving to others—thereby improving the quality of your relationships significantly.

Use Exaggeration to Diminish Self-Consciousness and Fear

Another reversal that can work wonders is to use exaggeration to reduce your self-consciousness in social situations.

Let's say that you're a shy person who is afraid to look foolish in public. You are self-conscious and think that everyone is always looking at you critically (judging you). Consequently, you may have what is called anticipatory anxiety. You are so afraid of appearing foolish in front of people—anticipating rejection and criticism—that you actually trigger more fear and anxiety in yourself, even before you engage in the social interaction.

To reverse the scenario, you can practice the exaggeration technique known as "Getting the Fools Out":

Exercise: Get Your Fools Out

In this exercise, you will "get your fools out"—you will intentionally act foolish and silly in an exaggerated way in private, so you can be more relaxed and confident in public.

Here's how it works: Get in front of your bathroom mirror. Decide that you will act like the biggest social fool in the world. Make weird faces in front of the mirror. Jump up and down like a kangaroo, howl like a wolf, laugh, sing, dance, stick your tongue out and yell, "I am the biggest social fool in the world. I am a weirdo. I am silly. I am foolish. Look at me."

You will say these things in a light-hearted, fun, and exaggerated way. You know you're not foolish or inadequate; you are just playing a role, much like a leading actor will choose a comedic role in which they play a buffoon for laughs. They know that, at the end of the day, the silly role they're playing is not who they are—it is just a role.

When you practice playing the fool in this way, you may feel uncomfortable at first, but gradually you will begin to relax and have a good time. You may even start to laugh heartily at your silliness.

More than just a fun exercise, Getting Your Fools Out has a practical purpose. By intentionally choosing to act like a fool in a private and controlled setting, you are giving yourself permission to make mistakes and look foolish (your biggest fear) in a social situation. Consequently, you are taking away most of the anxiety and self-consciousness that you normally associate with acting like a fool in public.

This is a liberating feeling. You can feel more confident when you do go out because you have used humor and exaggeration to reduce the anxiety you feel about being socially inadequate. Without self-consciousness, and the fear of being foolish holding you back, you are free to be your best self.

Use Reversal on the Money Game

This type of reversal—making a fun and exaggerated game out of what you're afraid of—can also be applied to any fear you have. Perhaps, you fear making a bad financial decision when investing; therefore, you procrastinate and don't make the investments you want to make.

To reverse your fear, take a small amount of money (something you can afford to lose) and say to yourself, "I'm going to learn how to invest with this money. It is my tuition. If I lose it, that's fine—that means I'm paying for my financial education."

When you see the money as an investment in your financial education, you will not be so fearful about losing it. You will have an entirely different attitude that will liberate you to learn more about finances and make the right investment decisions.

Overall, the key to bypassing frustrations and disappointments is to do the opposite of what you normally do. Instead of suffering from your fears, frustrations, and so-called weaknesses, embrace them, even exaggerate them. You do this so you can show yourself that you are in command of your weakness, instead of allowing your weakness to be in command of you.

Cultivate Reverse Giving

Reverse Giving means giving away what you most want to receive. It a powerful technique for dissolving your feelings of deprivation, envy, and frustration—the erroneous belief that the Universe is not giving you enough of the goodies in life. Reverse Giving works like this: If you want more wealth, give money and support to those who need it. If you want more love in your life, be more loving.

The power of Reverse Giving is that it works by merging the "giving" and "receiving" mentality until it is simply one unit—one comprehensive self-contained experience. When you do this, you become both the giver and the receiver at the same time. You give time, energy, and money to others, and you receive the feeling of compassionate helping and gratitude that you can be of service.

The interesting thing is that the giving and receiving part of the interaction happens at the same time. As you give the gift of listening to a suffering friend, you also receive the joyful feeling of gratitude that you can help your friend. It is a simultaneous and instant two-way expression of love—giving help to your friend and being grateful for being able to help—that can elevate you to a state of joy and contentment.

Wesley, a retired widower in his early-70s, felt lonely. He thought his children were too busy for him, he rarely saw his grandchildren, and his friends had gradually died off. He lived alone in a small apartment and often felt like a hermit. Although he felt the need for some type of affection and love, he didn't how to get it.

Fortunately, one of his friends introduced Wesley to the idea of Reverse Giving. He was told: "Wesley, if you want more love and attention in your life, why don't you try giving it to others first?"

After some reluctance, Wesley started visiting his grandchildren more. Even though he initially felt like he was imposing, his grandchildren loved it, and his grown children started to appreciate old dad around the house now that he was more accepting and less critical.

At the same time, Wesley felt the renewed love coming from his children and grandchildren. He recognized that the more love and attention he gave them, the more they gave back to him.

Wesley also joined a senior entrepreneur group that gave advice to young entrepreneurs. Soon he was making new friends and spending time with young people who reinvigorated him and kept his mind active. He was having a great time.

When you first start doing it, Reverse Giving may seem odd to you. Many of us are so accustomed to putting our own needs first that focusing on the needs of others (especially those who aren't in our inner circle) may seem alien to our nature. But the truth is that Reverse Giving is the most "selfish" thing you can do because you not only help others, but you can also reap many personal benefits: goodwill, material and spiritual benefits, and the satisfaction of knowing that you are making a positive contribution to the world. Whether it's love, money, or knowledge, giving away what you most want to receive can work wonders in your daily life. Even time can work in the same way. If you invest time in others, you will have more time. If you try to hoard it, you will have less of it.

Get Your Time Back

If you think about it, you will recognize that many people in modern society are time misers. They rush around trying to do more in less time, always complaining about their lack of time and how busy they are.

Here's the secret to reversing the game on time: To get more time in your life, give more of your time to others. Linger with a friend over a cup of hot coffee as you listen to their stories. Volunteer at a homeless shelter or help hotline. Spend more time with family or friends in nature outings, or just hang around the house playing games and laughing. It's an interesting paradox: Your time grows when you give it away by doing the things you love with the people you care about. When you do this, you enjoy life more, and you are more relaxed and unhurried.

You will be like a young child who feels they have plenty of time— time goes slowly. With this mindset, you can start to recapture that expansive and relaxed feeling of having abundant time; sitting outside in a sun-basked day, having nothing particularly important to do, except enjoying the moment.

This concept of giving what you want most—whether it's time, money, or energy—may sound intuitively appealing, but can be difficult for some people to practice. Many people are focused on receiving— money, love, approval, and material success. If they don't get what they want, they get frustrated and irritable. They are often gloomy, asking why the world gives to everyone else, but not to them.

Then, there are those people who are focused on giving, but do so because they want something in return: praise for their charitable works, or to make a good impression on other people. They proclaim loudly: "Look at how much of a giver I am. Look at me." They are under the mistaken impression that they are somehow better or more noble if they give to public causes—in reality, they only give to improve their image or receive accolades from others.

Finally, there are those people who are Reverse Givers—they give for the sake of giving; it is natural for them. They give from the bounty of their heart because a giver is who they are. As a result, they feel lighter, happier, and more loving. Their internal nature—love—has manifested itself outwardly in the form of external gifts to others, whether it is the gift of friendship, listening, financial support, or practical help.

Although they're not focused on getting something back from their giving, the truth is that they often receive an abundance from other people (and the world) because their good energy is usually returned in equal measure.

Exercises for Reverse Giving

Here are some ways to practice Reverse Giving:

- **Have a Generosity Week**: During the next seven days, focus on giving fully of yourself to others—not just money—but time, ener¬gy, advice, love, attention, and that rare, special gift: listening with a full heart—paying complete attention to what someone says without judgment. Many times, we don't listen fully to others; we are too busy thinking about what we're going to say to them. To listen fully and empathetically is a great gift that costs you little, but can enhance the lives of the people you listen to. They will feel appreciated and understood just because you listened without judgment.

When you practice giving outwardly to your loved ones, and even strangers, visualize your positive energy going out to shine on others. Think of it as a color; for example, green or yellow. Visualize it expanding outward as it shines a ray of loving light energy to the people you are directing your generosity toward.

With this new approach, you will notice that your previous feelings of frustration, anger, regret, and deprivation will vanish. In their place, you will experience feelings of newfound joy, peace, and satisfaction.

- **Have a Reverse Birthday**: On your birthday, you expect to receive gifts from family and friends. In this reversal, you will do something different on your birthday—instead of just receiving gifts, you will give gifts to your friends and loved ones.

  Depending on your budget, you can buy them drinks or food, give them small gifts, or do low-key things like giving them a massage, making them a homemade card or meal, or helping them with a practical matter or project (e.g. organizing their house). When you have a Reverse Birthday like this, you receive the greatest gift of all: The feeling of gratitude for all of the love and friendship you have received from those closest to you.

Reverse Giving is a special exercise. Although it may sound odd at first, it offers great power to change our way of thinking. Reverse Giving works by banishing our self-centered need to receive. It expands our mind by focusing on giving love and goodwill while receiving feelings of gratitude and love as a result of our giving.

When we want to receive something from others, whether it's material benefits, attention, or love, we are often afraid that we won't get what we want in exactly the way we want it. Thus, we live in anxiety and worry.

On the other hand, when we give with true generosity, there is no fear. We win regardless of whether someone accepts our gift or not. Our job is simply to give, and that is all.

As we extend our loving energy outward, we replenish our own inner store of power and love. It is a law of nature: What goes out must also come in. When we give love, we receive the same in return.

Be Grateful for the Bad as Well as the Good

While Reverse Giving is a powerful reversal, there are other useful reversals that can make a positive impact on your life. One of them is known as "Being grateful for the bad that happens to you as well as the good." Although few people want pain or bad things in their life, once they do come into your life, you can change the way you feel about them. You can start to see the good lesson in the pain; the new strength you can generate from the suffering.

It's like what happens when someone close to us dies. At first, we feel the pain of the loss. We grieve, we cry, we feel anguish and despair. But, then, we start to realize that there is a lesson to be learned from the death.

Aside from celebrating the life of your loved one, and seeing how their good qualities live on, you can also take valuable lessons from their departure. Perhaps, you will get into better physical and mental shape because you realize that life is short and fragile. Or, you will pay more attention to pursuing your dreams instead of waiting for later (if you die, later will never come). And, you won't take life for granted as much. You will realize how valuable time is. You will spend your time doing the most important things in life. You will help others and spend quality time with the people you love—telling them that you love them.

Once you truly realize that life is finite—you too are going to die—your entire perspective on life changes. You become more focused on living in the moment and relishing every experience of life. Whether you're skydiving for the first time, traveling to an exotic country, telling someone you love them, creating a beautiful work of art, teaching your children good values, or helping the poor on behalf of a nonprofit organization—you are fully and unabashedly alive. With this new awareness of the beauty of life, you do everything with more joy and gratefulness. You fully cherish each moment you have with the people you care about.

To Be Invincible, First Rid Yourself of What is *Not* Invincible

The final reversal you will learn is one of the most powerful: To be Invincible, rid yourself of what is *not* Invincible, especially Self-Defeating thoughts that try to keep you down.

As you start to eliminate the Self-Defeating attitudes from your mind, it is likely that you will encounter resistance. The Self-Defeating thoughts have been in your mind a long time. They are "mental squatters" who have grown comfortable trespassing on the sanctity of your mental palace. To evict them from your mind, you need to apply the reversals we will be talking about. In time, you will grow more comfortable without them, as you realize that they were only mental parasites living off the goodness of your true, Invincible mind.

Here are some common Self-Defeating mindsets you can eliminate to help you reach your Invincible Mind:

***The Need for Perfection:** Being Invincible doesn't mean that you're "Perfect," that you don't have any flaws. It means that you strive to be the best you can be, *despite* your flaws, weaknesses, or mistakes.

When you have a perfectionistic mindset, you do a disservice to yourself because you put yourself in a position of weakness. You become so fixated on not making a mistake that you become distracted and inflexible—thereby leaving yourself vulnerable to making the mistake you dreaded.

Start by deciding that you will do things at least 90% perfect. Not 100%, not 110%, but 90%. You can start with an even lower number if you like, perhaps 80%. You will do something well enough, for now, 80 to 90% perfect, while realizing that your goal is to complete the task and move on to the next one. With this new psychological approach, you forgive yourself if you are less than perfect, and you realize that a lower number gives you room for improvement each time.

Paradoxically, when you lower your need for perfection, while still maintaining good standards, you will find that you can perform even better because you have removed the tension and pressure of trying to be perfect.

Rid yourself of the need to be perfect, and you will have a new sense of Invincibility that rises above both perfection and error.

***The Belief That You Are Your Thoughts:**

Here is an interesting reversal: You are *not* your thoughts.

What this means is that a negative thought can come through your mind, but you don't need to "be" that negative thought. You can simply see it as a momentary flash that passes through your mind, but that has nothing to do with the essential "You," the higher Invincible You.

Your true identity as a strong and loving human being can be separate from any negative thoughts that momentarily course through your mind. Consequently, you don't have to suffer from attacking thoughts that compel you to act in a self-defeating manner. You can be mentally free at any moment in your life when you realize that the negative thoughts that temporarily enter your mind have nothing to do with the real you.

Unfortunately, a tremendous amount of pain and suffering have been created in the world when people have identified with negative and destructive thoughts—mistakenly believing that these malevolent thoughts were an integral part of their personalities. Throughout history, there have been times when entire nations have identified with thoughts of hate and discrimination toward others who were different—resulting in horrible actions that resulted in torture, murder, and genocide.

Things would be much different on earth, and in our individual lives, if we would realize that we are something higher, cleaner, and purer than our negative thoughts. The truth is that you are a free person who doesn't need to be compelled to suffer from fear, sadness, regret, or futility.

Label these negative entities as "Self-Defeating Thoughts," and let them pass through your mind without paying any attention to them. Realize that they are just momentary intruders who have nothing to do with the real Invincible You.

Kick them out of your mind—once and for all.

*The Belief That You Are What You Think You Must Obtain: This is another fallacy. You are not the sum of the things you want. If your mind tells you that you must have money, power, security, sex, approval, or romantic love to be happy, it doesn't mean that you are something if you get these things—and it doesn't mean that you are nothing if you don't.

Of course, you may want things, people, or circumstances to turn out in your favor, but your identity and essential nature don't need to be harmed if you're not able to obtain exactly what you're looking for. Just as your thoughts don't need to define you, what you want in life doesn't need to define you.

If you let outward things assert their control over you, then you will suffer if you don't get what you want in exactly the way you want it, or if you later lose it once you obtain it. A better way to live is to decide that you may want something to happen to you in life, but you will be perfectly fine if you don't get it in exactly the way you wanted it.

You realize that you are still a valuable human being even if you don't gain the exact amount of money you were looking for; if you don't win the heart of that particular lover; if you don't have the social approval of everyone you want it from. Although these things may bring you pleasure and satisfaction, you recognize that your essential Invincible nature, your true soul essence, resides at a loftier place that is above temporary advantages or benefits.

You may not realize it at the time, but reality (God/nature) will bring you exactly what you need when you need it. At first, you may be disappointed that you didn't receive the raise you were expecting; that your relationship didn't work out the way you wanted it to; that the business didn't make the money you thought it would. Yet, when your Invincible Mind is guiding you, you also recognize that there is something much greater in store for you: better relationships and career opportunities; greater business ventures and personal successes. All you have to do is place yourself on the side of your own Invincibility.

Your Invincible Mountain Peak

As you continue to make progress in your inner development, you will begin to experience the wonderful feeling of elevation from your Invincible Mind, from your journey to the top of Invincible Mountain—the place where joy, serenity, power, and love abound.

Although you may find mental potholes and weeds along the way, the tools you are learning will help you cut through the obstacles so you can achieve your ultimate destination of emotional excellence and psychological Invincibility.

Try this exercise: Imagine yourself standing on a mountaintop where the skies are blue and clear and the air is invigorating. On this mental mountain peak, you have a sense of joy, fulfillment, and love. You realize that the most important thing in life is to increase your Invincible state of mind so you can be free of self-defeating thoughts and actions. So you have the inner power to help yourself and others.

As you look out across the Invincible Mountaintop, you are pleased to see that there are other smiling and happy people who are comfortably perched on their own mountain peak. You feel a psychological kinship with these individuals who are striving to become Invincible, and who want to help others reach the same state of joy and fulfillment.

At the same time, you feel compassion for the frantic activity and anguish of your fellow human beings on earth who suffer under the weight of their Self-Defeating Minds. They feel trapped and believe they can't get out, no matter how hard they try. They suffer immensely from their own weakness.

Although you feel empathy for these individuals who are in pain, you also realize that everyone must make the climb to Invincible Mountain for themselves. You can offer advice and guidance to others, but each human being has to decide for themselves that they want to make the journey up the mountain, by themselves. Their friends, associates, collaborators, and even loved ones, can't make the journey for them. They need to be the ones who take the beautiful path toward personal invincibility.

Once a human being decides to take the upward journey, with sincerity and commitment, nothing can stop them. Not social disapproval, not shame, not regret, not sadness, not futility, not anger, not fear. Nothing can stop them.

And, nothing can stop you when you decide that you want to take the upward path toward Invincibility. When you reverse your priorities and place the most important thing first—Invincibility—everything else will be added to you, including loving relationships, rewarding work, meaningful experiences, excellent health and finances, enjoyment, fun, pleasure and happiness. It will be given to you as a bonus because you have put the most important thing first: your inner worth as a human being.

In the end, you will be Invincible, and you will rejoice in the truth:

You will stand as a rock. You will be indestructible. You will break your chains. You will be free forever.

Chapter Eighteen

....

The Power of Spontaneity

Spontaneity occurs when you are authentic—when you say and do what comes naturally for you. When you are spontaneous, you think quickly and flexibly; you react with an innovative response to a new situation. Spontaneity is a powerful force for your inner development. It is the energy behind joy, creativity, and laughter; it is one of the greatest tools you can use to help you live the Invincible Life.

Who is spontaneous in our busy, hurried, "You're important or not" world? Children and animals of course. They are able to easily tap into the energy of spontaneity. They jump, they play, they laugh (or bark or meow). They have a great time being in the moment—being playful, creative, and affectionate. They can be happy with a stick, a doll, a rock, and a little mud. That is all they need.

What happens when we become adults? The fun for some people consists of sitting in front of a small or big screen, putting food or chemicals into their bodies, and engaging in often pointless chatter. Perhaps watching a ball game or going shopping. Of course, there's nothing inherently wrong with a little technological entertainment, a sporting event, or shopping. But, much of what we call entertainment is contrived, artificial, and not all that much fun if you really think about it.

Moreover, as adults, we often tend to become rigid in our routines. We take the same route to work, vacation at the same place, eat at the same restaurants, make love in the same way, and live our lives predictably. As a result, we can become bored, stiff, and stifled.

How do we recapture our childhood spontaneity to live more freely and have more fun? By learning how to be more flexible, open to new experiences, and tolerant of changes in life. By taking ourselves less seriously, being more experimental, and having a "Why not?" attitude toward trying new things.

Although it's important to be responsible and serious about certain things in life such as engaging in ethical and moral behavior, and fulfilling our commitments as productive members of society, it is equally important to know when to let loose and have fun. To erupt with a deep belly laugh, make silly faces, sing and dance, and engage in playful activities with excitement and a sense of adventure.

Let's look at some ways to bring more of the magic of spontaneity into your life:

Play with Animals and Children

One way to be more spontaneous is by spending quality time with animals and children—some of the most fun and spontaneous beings on earth.

When you go to a child, they don't enter your world; they draw you into their world. They want to play, explore, and have fun. Join the fun and throw a ball with them, play with sticks or dolls; play imagination games, roll around in the mud; get silly. Animals are similar; they just love to have fun with you—running, jumping, and always ready for adventure.

Spending time with animals and children will have you smiling and laughing, and also getting some good exercise, as you let loose of your adult concerns and responsibilities. When you do this, you will see that your mood is lighter, and you don't take small things—petty disagreements or mechanical malfunctions—as seriously as you did before. The world becomes a happier and more fun place for you to be.

Play Spontaneously with Your Friends

Another way to recapture your spontaneity is to join some friends for improv or theatre games (games that actors use to improve their spontaneity).

A fun exercise is called "Build a Story." Go around your circle of friends (two or more) and create a story—one word at a time. The rules are a) the story must make sense, b) the participants need to listen carefully to the person who just said a word, and c) they must say the first word that comes to mind.

Here's the important ingredient: You can't think of what word you're going to say before you say it. It must come to you spontaneously.

For example, a word sequence could go like this:

"The...man...took...a...dog...to...the...beach...and...kissed...it... but...the...girl...had...a...dog...too...and...they...met...and... they...and...their...dogs...lived...happily...ever...after."

It doesn't matter how silly the story is as long as it makes some kind of sense. At first, the stories may not make any sense, or they may start out cohesively, but then degenerate into "mumbo jumbo," or nonsense. That's OK, just keep practicing. Initially, some of the participants may be nervous about what they're going to say, and they may overthink it—thus sounding artificial. But, as they become more confident and spontaneous, they will say the first word that comes to mind, and their stories will get more interesting and funny.

Try this spontaneity exercise with your friends, and you will find that your spontaneity and funny muscles will be strengthened. You will have a great time, and you will see yourself getting closer with your friends.

There is nothing more joyous than letting yourself go—from your adult preoccupations and your self-image of having to do things the adult and responsible way. Recapture some of your childhood spontaneity, and you will experience relief from the boredom and stress of your adult life.

As you begin to express your spontaneous nature, you will also increase your flexibility, openness to experience, and tolerance for differences in life. As a result, you will be lighter, as well as more fun-loving and productive.

Let's take a look at how mental flexibility can make a big difference in your level of happiness and success in life.

Play All the Keys on the Mental Piano

Think of your mind like a piano that has 88 keys. Each key on the mental piano represents an emotion; perhaps anger, fear, love, compassion, gratitude, or joy.

As you study this mental piano, you realize that one of the best ways to get out of an emotionally stuck place (anger or sadness) is to "play all of the keys on the mental piano"—to experience many different kinds of feelings: happiness, joy, gratitude, compassion, and so on.

On the other hand, people who are mentally ill, or have a serious psychological issue, often play the same key over and over again—getting caught up in fixed and repetitive mental patterns that lead them to negative emotions such as sadness, regret, or anger. Their one-note response to life often leaves them feeling frustrated and dissatisfied, as they keep repeating the same things:

"Nobody cares about me."

"There are problems everywhere."

"People (or society) are out to get me."

"I hate life."

The life of the mentally unhealthy person, therefore, often revolves around a few unpleasant propositions such as fear, guilt, selfishness, and the inability to forget. As a result, they narrow their mental repertoire—the way they live on a daily basis—until their entire mental world becomes one long endless noise.

Mental health, on the other hand, consists of broadening, instead of narrowing, your mental repertoire. It is based on improving on your abilities and talents and sharing them with the world.

Invincibility takes it one step further and asks that you become a virtuoso psychological piano player who can play all of the keys on the piano—from anger to forgiveness, sorrow to joy, and self-interest to compassion.

Being versatile in expressing your emotions can also make you a more well-rounded and confident human being. Research shows that people who have emotional granularity—the ability to describe their emotions accurately and with specificity—often have better psychological health. According to research cited in *Current Directions in Psychological Science*, people who have more emotional granularity engage in less binge drinking, aggression, and self-injurious behavior (Kashdan, Barrett, & McKnight, 2015). They also show less sensitivity to rejection and experience less severe anxiety and depressive disorders.

As a complete psychological piano player, you are not only aware of your emotions, but you are also able to choose the emotional notes you want to play on a daily basis—optimism, compassion, patience, intuition, creativity, and so forth. By choosing the emotions you want to have in your mind, you become the writer of your own song: a wonderful melody of wellbeing and peace.

Let's say that you're feeling sad about a health issue you're facing. Maybe, the health crisis is due to an accident or illness, and you feel depressed because you believe you won't ever be the same again. In the midst of this "key of sadness," you recognize that there are many other psychological keys you can play. You will focus your mind on positive and life-affirming thoughts: gratitude for your blessings, faith in recovery, love for your loved ones, and joy in recognizing the beauty of life.

Once you choose to play these positive thoughts in your mind, your mood will brighten, and hope will shine again in your heart. You will have the ability to broaden your emotional reactions to life—choosing to play positive and heartening psychological keys even when you face difficulty and pain.

Before long, you will become a virtuoso psychological piano player. Instead of being stuck in ingrained bad thoughts, emotions, and habits, you are able to create beautiful music that sounds lovely all of the time.

It is the music of Invincible You.

Enjoy the Easy Roll of Life

It's time to relax now and enjoy the "easy roll of life." What does this mean? With this perspective, instead of chasing people or circumstances, you let the things you want come to you naturally.

It works like this: Imagine that what you want in life—a person or circumstance—is a rock. A rolling rock that is up on a hill, while you are down below. If the rock rolls downhill toward you, you will enjoy it while you have it: the relationship, the money, the career opportunity.

But, here's the secret: You don't claim it as yours, or try to push it closer to you. You just let it roll as far as it wants to.

In the real world, this means that you don't try to force a person or circumstance to come closer to you. If you do so, you will likely end up feeling frustrated and disappointed. Instead, you will let the rock (person or situation) roll toward you as far as it wants to come. That is the easy way to live. There is no strain, worry, or anxiety.

If the rock should stop rolling toward you anywhere along the way—if the person stops calling, if the business opportunity dries up—don't try to push it further. Don't be upset or angry if the rock (person, circumstance) doesn't want to come any closer. It's not up to you whether it rolls toward you in the first place, or whether it stops; it's up to nature (God, reality).

If the thing you want stops rolling toward you, then look around. There are other rocks, or life circumstances, that you can follow. Enjoy their easy roll.

The problem for many people is that they try to control the rock; they try to push it their way. As a result, they end up fighting an uphill battle. The person you want doesn't want you. The money you seek is unavailable. The life circumstances you crave elude you. The rock is not coming toward you, and you feel disappointment, frustration, and anger.

What should you do when the rock stops rolling toward you—when the relationship or financial opportunity no longer works for you? There are a couple of approaches you can take.

One, you can give the rock a small nudge to get it rolling back down the hill again. You may undergo relationship counseling or seek advice on the financial matter. If it works, then the rock may roll toward you again.

But, perhaps after doing your due diligence, a particular rock of life still doesn't want to keep rolling in your direction. If that's the case, then you have a second option: Stop following the rock. Realize that it may be time to follow another rock—to move into a new relationship or financial opportunity.

Regardless of what happens, it's important to recognize that your results will be much better when you stop chasing the rock. You will be happier and more successful if you let the rock—the desirable person or circumstance—come to you. In this way, you will be in the flow of life; what you really need comes to you, naturally and effortlessly.

Of course, it's good to have goals, focus, and desires, but it's equally important to harmonize your desires with the dictates of nature and your ultimate path. When you do that, you realize the truth: No person can take the rock—what you want—away from you.

Only reality or God/nature can take it away, but that is usually for your own good, not your harm. When something is taken from you that doesn't truly belong to you, the very rejection of the wrong thing often opens the door for an even greater benefit or advantage to come to you in its place.

Exercise: Let Life Happen

Here's an exercise to help you learn how to follow the rock of life:

Go a single day without trying to force things to happen the way you wish or desire in life. Go about your business while letting everything happen the way it wants to happen. Refrain from trying to influence anyone or anything to turn in your desired direction. Instead of being a Doer, be a quiet Follower of everything that happens.

If you find yourself in a traffic jam, use the extra time to meditate and think about a great idea. If someone turns you down for a business proposition, consider that you may find an even better deal elsewhere. If the person you're romantically interested in doesn't feel the same, decide that you will find someone even more compatible and wonderful to be with. Whatever happens, go with it, and decide that you will be content no matter what happens.

Your resistance to letting life happen, naturally and spontaneously, often comes from the fear that things will not turn out the way you want them to unless you exert maximum effort. You may feel that you have to control everything to make sure things turn out right. While maintaining focus and determination are important in reaching your goals, there are times when relaxation and waiting are the best approach to take. Like a river that flows naturally into the ocean, you can relax and simply ride the currents of your life—trusting in your higher guide (God, nature) to take you to the right destination.

Once you are fully a Follower of the natural course of events, you become a Creator as well. With your new relaxed and flowing mindset, you will actually be more creative because your mind is free of unnecessary worry and strain. You bypass the nervous need to beat the clock; to rush around trying to get things done in an ever-decreasing amount of time. You drop the notion that you have to chase desirable people or favorable circumstances—you relax and let them come to you.

At this point, you can open your Intuitive Mind, your Hara, and allow it to receive higher impressions from God or nature. These higher ideas will tell you exactly what you need to do to achieve success in your personal and career/business ventures. Like many of our greatest artists, businesspeople, scientists, and thinkers have discovered, intuition and creativity often strike them when they least expect it.

Here are some examples of successful people who have experienced "aha" moments of intuition and inspiration that helped them come up with big solutions for life problems:

Jan Koum, an immigrant and engineer, wanted to call back home regularly to speak to his family in Ukraine, but he didn't have the money to do so. As a result of his personal need, he was inspired to come up with a free application, WhatsApp, for people to call internationally and keep in touch with their friends and families.

Lauren Bush Lauren, a former fashion model, was inspired by an idea to sell handbags and feed the hungry. Each handbag she sells has a number stamped on it that signifies the amount of meals provided with its purchase. Over 100 million meals have been donated to needy people through her company, FEED.

Mohammed Yunus was an economics professor who was frustrated by the cycle of poverty he saw in his native Bangladesh. He came up with the idea of micro-lending—making small loans to impoverished people—and won the Nobel Peace Prize for his contributions to humanity.

Debbie Sterling, an engineer by training, noticed that there was a lack of engineering toys targeted toward girls. As a result, she created GoldieBlox, a multimedia company that empowers girls to be interested in engineering and technology. Along the way, she created the world's first girl engineer character.

Like some of the creative and successful people just mentioned, you can accomplish great things and live happily if you allow your intuition to guide you as you flow with the rolling rock of life. The circumstances your desire, and the ideas you seek, will come to you when you're in tune with the rhythms of nature.

Take a Spiritual Vacation

As you flow with the rock of life, you will notice that your days become easier and more productive. Yet, despite the improvement, there will be times when you feel stuck, tired, and even frustrated. The rocks don't roll your way, and you wonder what you can do to change things.

When your energy flow is interrupted like this, you need to do something different. You need to take a Spiritual Vacation—a state of mental relaxation in which you go through your day as if you were on an actual physical vacation. In this relaxed state of mind, you enjoy every moment of every day as you participate in life with joy and power.

The truth is that many of us take life too seriously, so intensely, that we miss all the fun in it. A different view is needed: Think of life like a spiritual vacation. If you measured the time you have on earth, maybe 80 or 90 years, and compared it to eternity, that would be like a 24-hour vacation, or even a few minutes, before you have to go back. Unlike a work vacation, you don't know how long your "life vacation" will last. When the Big Boss calls you back, and your life is over, you've got to go, no matter what. You have to give up your body, your possessions, your loved ones, your life—everything.

If life is so short and unpredictable, then why not match its rhythm instead of fighting it? Some people try to ignore their mortality; pretending like death doesn't exist, and numbing themselves with exciting distractions and pleasurable activities such as eating, drinking, and socializing. Others do the opposite and fret about their future death; worrying about all of the unknown aspects of life and death. They are constantly asking the question: "What will happen to me?" "What will become of me?"

On the other hand, when you flow with life and match its rhythm, you harmonize with the moment and live spontaneously. You are content, regardless of what happens to you. Whether you gain or lose a relationship, career opportunity, or material possession, you are still happy. Deep down, you know there is always something better in store for you. You have a firm belief that God (Universe/reality) will provide everything you need.

At the same time, you realize that you don't know how long your spiritual vacation, your time on Earth, will last. When it's your time to go, it's time to go. With this realization, you will decide to live with full intensity, involvement, and passion. You won't wait too long to do what you've always wanted to do. You will act now.

Start today to fulfill your dreams and leave a lasting legacy of love and contribution. Live spontaneously and squeeze the last juices out of life until the heavens sing with joy. Life is your ultimate vacation; enjoy it.

Chapter Nineteen

....

The Final Key—Extend Loving Energy Without Expectation

There is a secret key to success in life. It is called Extend Loving Energy *Without Expectation*: Be kind and nice to others without expecting anything in return. This is the greatest love of all, and one of the greatest powers in the Universe.

When you love without expectation, you liberate yourself from the pain of unfulfilled expectations—the nagging thought that other people are not giving you the attention and love you deserve. Instead of trying to get something from other people, you are content within yourself. As a result, you attract the right people and circumstances that resonate with who you really are.

Although loving without expectation can convey many benefits, the reality is that many people love conditionally. They love others while wanting something back from them. They want their love, sex, companionship, money, support, approval, or agreement with their point of view.

Of course, these things can be nice to obtain from a loved one, or people we respect; however, the truth is that we will not always receive what we want from those we care about. In the real world, your partner may love you less than you love them. Others may not give you the accolades, approval, and "warm fuzzies," you seek.

Now what? It's time to consider the power of Loving Without Expectation.

Be Like the Sun: Love Without Expectation

To be successful in life, one of the greatest secrets you can apply is to Be Like The Sun: Wherever you go, be like the sun and radiate your goodness and loving warmth to all—without expecting anything in return. By doing so, you will bring people and circumstances into your life that harmonize with the real you.

Think about it: The sun shines on everything and everyone—the young, the old; the rich, the poor; the kind, the unkind. Some people don't like the sun and cover themselves up, while others love it and will lie down to soak up its rays. Yet, no matter what, the sun remains the same: It keeps shining its light and warmth because it is the sun.

Do the same and radiate your positive and loving energy to everyone, without worrying about what you're receiving back from them. You will smile at them, mentally extend your positive energy, help them, and give them appreciation and feedback without expecting anything in return—not even a smile or acknowledgement.

You do this because you are powerful like the sun. You don't base your existence or value on other's approval, or liking, of you. Like the sun, you are a force of nature that expresses your loving energy to all who surround you. As a result, you become stronger and brighter regardless of other's reactions to you; whether they are positive or negative.

When you extend loving energy like this, your thinking becomes a fixed power. You don't waste time thinking about who doesn't like you, or what doesn't work in life. You don't worry about the idea that others will reject you, or that you will feel abandoned and unloved.

Instead, you place yourself in a focused, relaxed, and receptive frame of mind that will naturally attract what you need: meaningful relationships, successful career ventures, and fulfilling life experiences.

Always remember to be like the sun. Keep shining your positive and loving energy to the world, no matter what. By doing so, you will not only improve the lives of others, but you will also uplift your own life as well.

What if the One I Love Doesn't Love Me Back?

Now you may be wondering: Although loving energy without expectation sounds like a nice idea in theory, what happens when the one I love—whether friend, family member, or potential love partner—doesn't have the same feelings for me? There is great pain. What do I do then?

If that happens, you will still extend loving energy without expectation. You won't expect that they will like you, or will be interested in you, or even that they will give you much attention. You will simply exude positive and loving energy outwardly in the vicinity of this person because that is who you are inside: You are made of loving energy.

As you extend loving energy without expectation like this, there is never anything to worry about. If the person you are offering love and interest to resonates with your style and nature, then your loving energy stays with them—they will naturally be interested in getting closer to you.

On the other hand, if their energy is different, and their desire reigns elsewhere, then your loving energy will return to you. You have lost nothing. Regardless of the reason why they don't respond to you, you will not be offended or hurt when your energies don't connect. You will simply extend your loving energy without expectation elsewhere—to a place or person where it will be reciprocated and sent back to you.

Think of your loving energy like a yo-yo that you toss to someone: Either they catch it, or they don't.

If they catch your loving energy, you have created a solid connection. If they don't catch it, then the yo-yo, your loving energy, returns to you. There is nothing lost. The loving energy belongs to you and always did.

With this new mindset, you eliminate the middleperson, otherwise known as Expectation—the hardened notion that you must receive something in return for your energy and affection. Without the troublesome Expectation crawling around in your head, you are free to simply receive whatever the person is willing to give, or not give to you.

No matter what happens, you have a light, free, and loving feeling toward the person, even if they don't respond to you in a loving manner. You realize that there is no greater love than to be able to love others without being affected negatively if they don't love you back.

Of course, you may ask, "What happens if they just take my love and abuse it?" If this happens, you will operate by a guiding principle: You will only keep extending loving energy as long as your love is doing good. If there is non-acceptance, or misuse, of your loving energy by the other person, then you will simply relocate your energy.

If others don't want it, or if they abuse what you are offering, then you will simply extend your loving energy in another direction. You do this without feeling angry, rejected, or resentful. You will be like the sun that shines its light on everyone. The sun doesn't get mad or upset if people cover up from its rays; it just keeps shining. You will do the same.

Extending loving energy without expectation doesn't mean that you're a fool or martyr. It doesn't mean that you allow others to humiliate you or take advantage of your kindness. When you give loving energy to others, you will be as wise as a serpent, but as harmless as a dove. Ultimately, your love will be deposited in the right hands, and you will be rewarded a thousandfold in terms of love, goodwill, and good fortune being returned to you.

How to Be Nice the Right Way

You may be thinking, "I already show love to others. I'm nice to people and they take advantage of me. They think I'm weak and take me for granted. Why should I keep being nice?"

That's a good question. While it's a common phrase that "Nice people finish last," that's not entirely true. Nice people—those who are kind, patient, loving, and forgiving—can be among the strongest, most successful, and most loved people on earth. As we examine this topic, it's important that we first define what type of "nice" we are talking about. There are different varieties of "nice."

If you're nice to yourself, and not to others, you are considered selfish. You only want what you want, and you don't care what others think. A selfish life often becomes a lonely life because quality people will avoid individuals who only care about themselves. There is a lack of mutual connection—ultimately resulting in no connection at all.

If you're nice to others, and not nice to yourself, then you may become a self-induced victim, also known as a false martyr. The false martyr is someone who loves playing the self-sacrificial role because it enhances their ego ("Look at all I sacrifice for you/others"). Usually, this person is taken advantage of by others who see their overly giving nature as a weakness they can exploit.

Another combination is when you're nice to neither yourself nor others. This is a miserable human being—the type of person who is negative, pessimistic, and cynical. They have given up on the good values of hope, faith, and optimism. These sad individuals often pity themselves and go around complaining about how much life and others have destroyed them. They are harsh to themselves and critical of others. Unfortunately, once they are stuck in this mindset, it is very difficult to get them out of it.

The ideal way in life is to be nice to yourself and others: Treat yourself and others with kindness and respect. In this way, you are a genuinely nice human being.

Being nice, however, doesn't make you weak or inferior. On the contrary, a truly nice person is very strong inside. They are strong because they are authentic, caring, and helpful from their core—from who they are inside. They don't need to maintain a false façade of niceness in hopes that other people will like them, or approve of them. Their niceness is merely an outward projection of what they already possess internally; they are content within themselves.

Truly nice people know when to be firm, and when to be tough. They don't let Negativity Seekers take advantage of them. They realize that being firm with people who are struggling with their own minds is often the best way to help them.

Rather than giving in to other people's neurotic or unrealistic demands, truly nice people know that real compassion can sometimes consist of a quick kick in the psychological pants—to motivate the misguided individual to change, instead of coddling their insecurities and weaknesses.

At the same time, the truly nice human being is not only nice to others, but they are also nice to themselves.

Being tolerant and nice to yourself means forgiving yourself for any real or imagined errors you may have made in life. It means taking care of your mind, body, and soul: exercising, eating right, engaging in a spiritual or life-affirming practice. When you have true loving feelings toward yourself, you will project those feelings outwardly toward others in a natural way that is devoid of calculation and manipulation.

Think about it: How can a person who is cruel and unjust to themselves be anything other than the same to others? Cruelty projects itself outwardly as does kindness. You can only give to others what you have inside—a hot teapot can only pour hot tea. If you condemn and judge yourself, you will do the same to others; if you forgive and love yourself, you will do the same for others.

Your ultimate goal is to be a nice person who is also real. There is no fakery in your niceness; it is 100% authentic. Ultimately, your goodness and human quality of excellence will naturally attract other like-minded people into your life. Together, you can work together for the common good to bring more peace, harmony, and love into the world.

How Loving Energy Can Banish Fear

Being nice, kind, and loving is not just to improve your relationships with others; it can also help you achieve greatness within yourself. It can help you overcome negative emotions such as Fear—one of the biggest stumbling blocks of humanity.

Here's an important idea: There is no fear in giving; there is only fear in taking.

When you want something from others, or from the world, you may fear that you won't obtain it, or that you will lose what you already have. This can make you feel tense, worried, and ultimately disappointed if things don't work out the way you expected.

On the other hand, when you extend loving energy outwardly without expectation, you have no fear because you don't expect anything in return. If you don't expect anything, you can't fear any loss.

One of the most beautiful phrases ever written comes from the New Testament: "Perfect love casts out fear." In other words, a love dedicated to something higher bypasses fear. That something higher may be God or spiritual essence, a sacred connection between two loving partners, or the unconditional love between parent and child.

When a mother sees her young child trapped under a car and somehow lifts it to rescue her child, she practices the principle of perfect love casting out fear. Her desire to save her beloved child allows her to take quick action despite the fear she was experiencing.

Yes, it is true: Fear and love can't exist on the same plane. You can't feel both at the same time. Since love is stronger than fear, your best bet in life is to cultivate as much inner love as you can.

In fact, you will thrive the most when you are able to extend loving energy without expectation. This means that you will express your loving energy—smile at others, say nice words, help them—without expecting anything in return.

To heal and nurture yourself, your task is to shine your loving energy to everyone—men, women, children, animals, and even inanimate objects—for as long as you live. When you do this, you will release a refreshing and powerful energy within yourself that is difficult to define: a source of goodness and light that expands your life and improves the lives of those around you (even those you will never meet).

When you extend loving energy without expectation, you enter the mental kingdom of another. You see as they see; you feel as they feel. Also known as empathy or compassion, this is a powerful way to connect with, and extend, your loving energy to others. As you give loving energy to others, you are also giving it to yourself because you feel inside what you are giving out: Pure love.

The Secret of Why Dogs Are Loved

Why do so many people love dogs so much, sometimes even more than humans? Because dogs give love without expectation. No matter what happens, they are always there for you—attentive and loving; patient and devoted (except for a few of the fussier ones).

There are valuable lessons in loving energy without expectation that we can learn from our four-legged friends.

> *There once was a traveler who was looking for a hotel while he stayed in the city; he happened to be traveling with his Pomeranian dog, Misty. He emailed several hotels to see if they would accept his dog, but they all said, "No."*
>
> *Finally, one hotel owner responded as follows:*
>
> *"You ask if I accept dogs in my hotel. Yes, I do: I find them to be the most gracious of guests. I have never yet had a dog guest light a cigarette in the room and set one of our beds on fire. I have never had a dog guest get drunk and throw up all over the room after breaking everything inside. I have never had a dog guest get into such a contentious fight with their love partner that the police had to be called. Yes, I will say that your dog is a most welcome guest in our hotel. I would love to have her.*
>
> *PS: You can come too, if Misty says you're OK."*

Why are dogs so loved by many people? Because they offer unconditional love; always wagging their tails and jumping when they see their human friend; always happy to see you, no matter what. We can learn valuable lessons on how to be loved by studying the natural charisma of a dog.

Here are some personality characteristics of the dog that you can apply in your own life.

1. Be Interested in Others and They Will be Interested in You: Dogs are always interested in us, following us from room to room, constantly keeping their eye on what we're doing. As humans, we tend to be self-centered, always thinking about our own needs and how we are coming across.

To be loved, you need to do a reversal: Project interest outside yourself. Become genuinely interested in other people; ask them questions about their lives, what their passions are, how you can be of service to them.

Practice your empathy with waiters/waitresses, delivery people, or others who provide you with a service. Take time to talk to a new person at a coffeeshop or in a line at a store—make small talk, but also ask about their goals and dreams in life. Think about how others are feeling when you converse with them. Consider what makes them happy; what makes them sad.

When you do this, you expand your focus from your small "me world" (self-centered) into a larger perspective of connection, compassion, and empathy. You will find that people will be more interested in you because you have entered their world with a genuine desire to know more about them and connect with them.

2. Live Daily with Enthusiasm: Dogs often have unrelenting enthusiasm; they want to play, they want to go outside with you; they want to jump, wag their tail, and bark.

In our daily stressful and busy lives, we often forget to play—to have fun, laugh, and be spontaneous. Dogs are a good reminder that we need to get in touch with the playful and fun-loving side of our personality.

Tickle a friend, tell a joke on yourself, play a fun prank, go to a comedy show, or play a childhood group game (like "Simon Says") with your adult or child friends. When you do this, your face will become animated. You will smile and laugh more, and you will look more attractive, regardless of your facial and body features. People will want to spend more time with you because you are fun, interesting, and charming.

3. Do Something Nice for Others: Dogs have been known to bring slippers and newspapers for their human friends, lick their human friends on their faces when they are sad, and cuddle up to them when they are lonely.

You can model the dog's caring nature by doing nice things for others—helping a homeless person, listening to a hurting acquaintance, smiling and paying compliments to others. The secret is to be nice, without expecting anything in return—you don't need them to like you or give you an equal benefit.

What you will find is that the nicer you are to others, the nicer they will be to you. It may not even be the person you are nice to who is nice in return, but it could be someone else—a person you don't even know—who helps you when you least expect it.

You have just learned the three secrets of why dogs are loved. If you adopt these personality traits as your own, you will learn the dog's truth:

Be Interested in Others and They Will be Interested in You
Live Daily with Enthusiasm
Do Something Nice for Others

LoveQ: The New Intelligence That Will Change Your Life

As we get deeper into our study of loving energy, we realize that love is more than just a feeling, or even a state of mind. It is a form of intelligence; a power that can be used for the good of yourself and others.

You probably know about standard IQ: the ability to learn from experiences and adapt to changing environments. You may also have heard about Emotional Intelligence—successfully managing emotions and relationships.

Now there is a new form of intelligence which is called Love Intelligence, also known as LoveQ. Love Q is not just about being smart in relationships. It goes beyond that to encompass a psycho-spiritual way of being in which you fully maximize your potential on earth.

This LoveQ contains essential psychological and spiritual characteristics that make up a whole and healthy human being. These vital elements include compassion, empathy, kindness, patience, generosity, and gentleness, to name a few. When you have a high level of LoveQ, you understand yourself and others better, and you achieve more emotional balance and harmony.

By increasing your LoveQ, you also receive many real-world benefits. People who are high in LoveQ often are healthier, more productive at work, make more money, are better leaders, and are able to create better family, friend, and love relationships.

When you have a high LoveQ, you will initially feel love internally as an energy—a sense of compassion and empathy—as you realize the limits of human life and the boundless nature of the human spirit. Then, you externalize that energy through your positive relationships with people and the good works you are able to give to the world.

Imagine if we lived in a truly loving Earth where policemen, psychologists, armies, and weapons of destruction were essentially obsolete and eliminated. In this type of society, crime wouldn't exist. Before someone committed a crime or violent act, they would feel empathy toward the people who would suffer because of their actions, and they would abstain from doing so. Instead of violence and hatred, they would offer peace and compassion to others, and they would receive the same in return.

Simply put, love is the higher power, also known as God or nature, as manifested in human beings. It is an essence that surpasses mere words. What we do know is that love is the strongest force for good in the world. It has the capacity to bring people together from all nations and walks of life; to heal the hurting and bring peace and contentment to all who come under its influence.

Here's a beautiful truth: Even the briefest experience of love without expectation can transform you—giving you a glimpse into the meaning of a higher or universal love. This love transcends mere words and comes from a source that has many names: God, Creator, nature, essence, and spirituality.

True loving energy without expectation is a virtue the blind can see and the deaf can hear. As long as there is one person you can console by words, or enliven by your presence, then you are a precious possession to the human race. You can make a positive difference in the world, one person at a time.

When you experience love of this magnitude, your face will shine, and your heart will sing. You will be encompassed by an amazing feeling that is difficult to describe. With this type of love, you will experience many other positive emotions including compassion, gratitude, forgiveness, peace, and joy. You will be transformed from an ordinary human being into a person who is well on their way to having an Invincible Mind.

LoveQ Brings Daily Power

LoveQ may sound idealistic, and even fanciful to some, but it is actually a very practical and useful trait to have. With a high LoveQ, you will not only have better personal relationships, but you will also do better in business, moneymaking, health, and a dozen other practical issues.

For example, when you have a high LoveQ, you have an enhanced sense of empathy. Because you quickly see the position of other people, you can come to better agreements, deals, and understandings since others will sense that you have their best interests in mind. Consequently, you will have mutually beneficial business dealings, and you will make more money because people will want to work with you.

Also, when you raise your LoveQ, you operate at a high level of clarity and efficiency because your mind is not overly burdened with unfulfilled expectations—trying to get other people to like you, or to go along with you. You exude a natural higher intelligence that attracts the right people and circumstances into your life.

With a strong LoveQ, you also have stronger personal relationships because you exude a high level of compassion and patience—friends, family, and loved ones will want to be around you because you are supportive, loving, and kind-hearted.

Not only are you more loving toward others, but you are also more loving toward yourself. You will take better care of your health. You will make sure that you maintain the best diet, exercise, and sleep habits. As a result, you have more energy, and you will feel better than ever before.

LaWanda was a hard-driving corporate executive in her late-40s. She enjoyed her highly competitive job, but often drove her employees into a nervous state with her intense and perfectionistic demands (she had a high turnover rate in her department). Moreover, feeling stressed and time-pressured most of the time, she had a hard time sleeping at night—her mind was a frantic whirlwind of all the things she had to do.

Realizing that she wasn't as content or effective as she could be, she explored various models of self-development. Always interested in self-improvement, she started studying the concept of LoveQ and began to practice it.

She began by imagining that she was breathing in compassion for herself—forgiving herself for being less than perfect. Then, she continued by breathing out compassion for others—imagining that she was extending a type of loving energy outwardly to her family and loved ones, and then to her friends and work associates.

As she raised her LoveQ, she noticed that she was becoming more relaxed and productive. She was also eating healthier and sleeping better. In addition, she was pleasantly surprised to see that her employees were performing better and had a more positive attitude at work. They were picking up on her newfound positive energy and were modeling her new empathetic style.

Soon, she was breaking production records and experiencing something entirely new: She was excelling at work with a relaxed and loving mindset. She was increasing her LoveQ.

Like LaWanda, if you raise your LoveQ, you can enjoy more productivity at work, better relationships, and a more contented mind. You won't be as tormented by your old "Monkey Mind"—the chattering voices in your head that warn you about all the problems you will be facing. You will quiet the tormenting and repetitive thoughts that keep you worried about all the things you have to do. The people around you will also notice the difference as you become more compassionate, patient, and open-minded.

Here are some tools to help raise your LoveQ so you can enjoy this new and marvelous state of being:

Patience: The Selfless Way

One of the essential LoveQ elements is Patience—the ability to wait for the good things to come to you; to enjoy each moment with complete awareness. Patience is the glue of mental health—the mindset that prevents you from rushing into bad situations and unhealthy relationships because you know that the best things in life will come to you in due time.

Impatience, on the other hand, is inner restlessness. It is a compulsive desire to escape from the now; to have something exciting and stimulating going on at all times. The impatient person is rarely happy where they are in the present. Consequently, they are always looking to go to the next and better place, to meet the more attractive and charming person; to grab the bigger financial reward.

The impatient person also lives by the clock—always checking it to see if there is something they should be doing (there usually is). Unfortunately, impatience dulls a person's compassion—it plants the seeds of self-absorption and selfishness.

In big cities with modern technology, we may start to perceive human requests for companionship and assistance as interrupting plans for our free time. With an impatient mindset, we can lose our capacity to enjoy the people we live and work with—we are too impatient and busy to spend time with them.

When you live with patience, on the other hand, you live an entirely different life. You experience each moment as full and rich—realizing that there is ample time to live in its fullness. Living patiently is when you invite others to share in your seemingly endless time.

With patience, you are also more tolerant of people's flaws and weaknesses. You realize that human beings can have certain moods; sometimes cheery; other times grumpy, based on the circumstances. You understand that people and situations change over time—today's angry acquaintance can become tomorrow's loving friend. When you are patient, people respond better to you because they feel that you care about them and understand their point of view. In turn, they will be more likely to see your point of view and help you achieve your goals.

When you practice patience, you are not only becoming more patient with others, but also with yourself. You give yourself a break if you're not accomplishing your goals as quickly as you thought you would. You forgive yourself for any flaws or inadequacies you think you may have, while realizing it takes time for you to grow and develop as an Invincible human being. You take time out to take care of yourself—physically, emotionally, and spiritually. As a result of being patient with yourself, you love yourself more—not in a selfish or ego-centered way—but in a way that replenishes your energy and allows you to give more to others.

To become more patient, practice slowing down your pace in life. Try this exercise:

Exercise Your Patience Muscles

Think of patience like a muscle that you can make stronger by exercising it—by practicing patience on a daily basis.

Starting today, experiment with living a slower life. Eat slower, walk with full awareness of where you're going, take time off from work to socialize with friends, or to do something fun. Observe and model yourself after people who are patient, perhaps a contented elderly person. See how little in life bothers them; they know there is plenty of time for everything, and they are often calm in the face of difficulties.

When you first begin to develop patience, you will likely encounter resistance from your foe, the Rush Weakness, as it tries to frantically push you to act quicker, faster, more urgently—yelling at you that "Life is passing you by," and that you have "Already wasted too much time." Use the resistance of the Rush Weakness in your favor like a person who adds extra weights to improve their strength when working out. Every time you slow yourself down to savor the moment, and do things right, mark it as a win over the Rush Weakness. When you slow down, you will paradoxically achieve faster results because you maintain full awareness of everything you're doing and you cut down on the mistakes you have been making.

As you become more patient, you will find daily moments—small pockets of relaxation—in which you can practice your patient mindset. Perhaps, you will take a brief walk around your neighborhood or nearby park as you breathe deeply. Or, you may meditate in your backyard or park for a short period of time. You can also do some physical exercise or mindfulness exercises, or play with animals or children for a while. All of these activities will help you relax so you can focus on the joy of the present moment.

As you become more patient, you will find that you will enjoy a better relationship with yourself and others. With less stress and pressure in your mind from impatience, you can give yourself the time you need to nurture relationships and relish the special moments of your life.

The Miracle of Compassion

Another important element of LoveQ is compassion: the desire to relieve the suffering of others. When you have a high level of compassion, you realize that nobody is perfect in life, and that people suffer from their own nature (gloomy, depressed, critical). At the same, you realize that being compassionate to others will also help you heal from your own suffering. Your outward expression of compassion reflects itself inwardly in the form of self-love and self-forgiveness.

Here is a thought experiment to help increase your Compassion:

Exercise: Breathe Out Compassion

Begin by reflecting on the suffering of humanity. Think about couples as they go through a divorce, families caring for sick or dying children, animals, or parents; those who are struggling with financial problems, addictions, loneliness, or depression.

Now take a deep breath and visualize yourself inhaling all of the difficulties and pain of the people around you. Start with those closest to you, friends and family, and then spread out to your entire community.

After inhaling their troubles, visualize yourself exhaling peace, love, healing, and compassion. Exhale forcefully and slowly. Imagine that you are sending out a stream of loving energy with a certain color, perhaps blue or white. As you project this colored light to others, visualize that you are helping them heal from their maladies and problems.

Imagine that you are giving them your energy, talent, compassion, and love—flowing from you to them—to help them heal their wounds and bring light and positivity into their lives. Imagine that their tears are being dried, and their faces are now beaming with happiness as inner peace and serenity fill their lives.

Continue inhaling and exhaling, as you begin to empathize with the problems of the world. Inhale all darkness, disease, and unhappiness. Exhale with the thought: "May all beings receive my happiness, faith, and fearlessness."

At first, imagining that you're taking in the pain of others, and giving them all of your good, may seem overly self-sacrificial and even counterproductive. You may think: "I need to take care of myself and my family first before I give to others." Yet, the truth is that there is great benefit in doing this exercise. When you visualize yourself giving away your advantages, assets, and delights to others (even to those you don't know), you discover that you have abundance in your life. You realize that you have more positive resources to give than you can possibly imagine—you have infinite psychological and spiritual riches.

Now, look around and see where you can offer compassion to others in the real world. Assist the needy and disadvantaged. Give advice to a grieving person. Help a homeless person with basic necessities. Volunteer to be a good role model for children. Be a companion for elderly people who are lonely. On a daily basis, give more love to others.

With your heightened sense of compassion, you will also give more love to yourself; you will practice self-compassion. When you need a rest day, a mini-vacation, or a real vacation, you will take the time to regenerate yourself. You will take better care of your health—diet and exercise—so you can have a long and healthy life. You will forgive yourself for any mistakes you have made, and you will praise yourself, without arrogance or conceit, for all the good you have done in the world. At the same time, you will look forward to all of the good things you can still accomplish while you are still here on this Earth.

Empathy Building: Reversal of Destiny

Empathy is the ability to put yourself in someone else's shoes. It is a powerful tool for growth and understanding people, and is an important part of LoveQ. When you are empathetic to other people, you place yourself in their mindset and see the world as they see it. As a result, you can communicate with them in a way that connects at the deepest level of their desires, values, and goals. Because you can sense their joys, sorrows, excitements, and disappointments, you can clearly see what motivates them and what pushes them away.

As an empathetic person, you will be a better businessperson, friend, parent, partner, and citizen. You will have more solid relationships based on equity and mutual respect. You can persuade others to act for a higher good, and you can motivate and inspire them when they are down. Best of all, you will feel better about yourself because you are a caring and loving person who sees the world as an interconnected place—recognizing that, deep inside, we are all the same; we love, we laugh, we cry, and we want to live the happiest life possible with those we care about.

Here's an exercise to help you maintain that wonderful mindset known as empathy:

The Role Reversal Exercise

To increase your empathy, try this roleplaying exercise with a friend:

Step One: You will play the part of a homeless person who has just been robbed and beaten, while your friend acts like an arrogant and busy businessperson. Your friend, the arrogant wealthy person, will scoff at you, "You're faking it. You just want the spare change to get high. Get a job, loser."

Step Two: Switch roles as you become the arrogant rich businessperson, while your friend is the helpless homeless individual.

Step Three: Take turns going back and forth between the two roles—arrogant rich and humiliated poor—and jot down your thoughts and feelings as you experience each scenario.

Perhaps, you will initially feel angry when you are the homeless person who is being berated by the entitled snob. Then, when you switch roles and become the rich person, you may feel arrogant and powerful, and you may be tempted to return the animosity to your friend.

Or, the opposite may occur. When you move from homeless to rich, you actually may feel more humble, compassionate, and empathetic toward your roleplaying partner who is now homeless. You remember what it felt like to be beaten down and homeless when you were in that position, and you can feel the pain of your partner.

Eventually, your goal is to see the world and humanity from two perspectives at the same time. You will see yourself from the eyes of the rich person giving aid to the homeless person, and you will see yourself from the eyes of the homeless person receiving the help.

As the rich person, you are giving with gratefulness that you can help; as the homeless person, you are receiving the help with gratitude. When you see life from this two-way perspective, you are truly united to all human beings—you are able to extend loving energy to others as both the giver and the receiver. You realize that real love is selfless and free from fear. It pours itself out upon the object of its affection without demanding anything in return.

Raise Your LoveQ Daily

You have begun to take the right steps toward raising your LoveQ—one of the most powerful forces in the Invincible You life.

One of the best ways to increase your LoveQ is to practice giving love without expectation. As you do this, you will begin to see the evidence of love in many places. You will see it in a mother feeding her infant, a child saying goodbye to their beloved parent as they die, the joy of a couple in love holding hands, and the bliss of a believer worshipping a higher nature (God/spiritual essence).

When you become aware of these daily examples of loving without expectation (unconditional love), you will feel elevated and joyous. You will experience the beauty of this exalted state that goes far beyond mere mortal experience and life on earth. It is the only thing left when a loved one dies: The unconditional love you have for them.

Some people may think that LoveQ is an unrealistic concept—the fanciful and naive notion that we can all love each other and live in a peaceful and harmonious world. Perhaps it is somewhat idealistic to think that love can permeate the world. But, it is also very realistic because loving energy is a force that can be felt, it can be measured, and it can grow. Think of LoveQ like a type of equity that you can increase to add value to your life and the lives of others, much like you would increase the value of your home if you made improvements on it.

Yes, it's true: When you extend loving energy without expectation—and raise your LoveQ—you will be one step closer to living the Invincible Life and reaping many benefits:

- You will be inwardly peaceful when attacked by others.

- You will be relaxed and harmonious: You are no longer anxious and frustrated.

- You will love and do what you like—genuine love harms neither yourself nor others.

- Your relationships will be more loving.

- Your finances and health will improve.

- Your happiness will increase; you will genuinely love yourself and others without self-centeredness.

- You will clothe yourself with strength. You will put on your garments of splendor. You will shake off the dust. You will free the chains from your neck.

- You will be Invincible.

PART THREE

ON TOP OF INVINCIBLE MOUNTAIN

Chapter Twenty

....

Your Ultimate Questions Answered

We are nearing the end of the Invincible You journey, and I'm sure you have questions. Here, I will answer some of your most important questions to help you discover effective ways to reach your Invincibility.

The best way to apply this chapter is to digest a few questions and answers each day as you find yourself growing into the person you were meant to be.

Let's start with some pressing issues:

How to Handle People Problems

Q: *Other people bug me all the time. My main problems are always about people. They can be rude, obnoxious, selfish, deceitful, unfaithful, and manipulative. What do I do about my people problems?*

A: The answer to your people problems is simple: Get rid in yourself anything that you don't like in others.

If you're tired of vanity and lies in others, get rid of these traits in yourself.

If you're tired of selfishness in others, get rid of it in yourself.

If you're tired of rudeness and impatience in others, get rid of them in yourself.

Why? Because the people in your life are often a reflection of who you are inside.

A hammer and the sun have nothing in common with each other. One is an earthly tool meant to hammer things. The other is full of light and energy, and is elevated. If you are an aggressive person, you will find other hammers to fight with, and you will see other people as nails to be hammered. If you are like the sun, you will shine your positive energy on everything around you. Consequently, the hammers (aggressive people of the world) won't be able to bother you. They can't hurt you because you are far above their influence.

Instead of complaining about other people, strive to change yourself—to elevate yourself psychologically to a point where you are no longer disturbed by the bad behavior of others. Does the sun worry about people who shout at it in anger or fear? No, because the sun is at a much higher elevation. Be like the sun and place yourself at a higher place than the petty problems and negative people of the world.

Then, you will be a free human being who is no longer at the mercy of the whims of others who behave badly, and who demand that you be what they want you to be. You will be the only thing you were meant to be: Your true Invincible Self.

How to be Invincible

Q. You talk about "Invincibility." How can I be Invincible when there are so many other distractions in life, both from the outside world, and my own inner thoughts?"

A: Here are some simple exercises to bring more Invincibility into your life:

1. **Take a daily "mental bath" as you take an actual water bath.** As you bathe in a tub of warm water, or take a hot shower, visualize yourself getting rid of sick thoughts and accumulated negative energy from yourself and others.

2. **Shake with "Hands of Love."** Imagine that your hand contains hundreds of individual loving minds, each having an intelligence of their own. When you shake people's hands, imagine that you are passing loving energy to them through your hands.

3. **Breathe deeply when you are happy:** As you breathe, steady your mind and maintain full concentration. Associate breathing with happiness as you feel the happiness growing inside you.

4. **Concentrate your mental forces and attack at the point where you can achieve a breakthrough**. Find the one area where your improvement will yield immediate results in your life. For example, if procrastination is an issue for you, resolve that you will take one small action toward an important task. If regret bothers you, practice forgiving yourself for real or imagined errors. If loneliness is your weakness, resolve to give love to others without expectation. By choosing which psychological issue to focus on first, you will achieve a rewarding feeling of success that gives you the motivation and self-confidence to pursue new goals.

How to Get Ahead

Q: I try to improve myself, but I always screw up. Then I find myself in a worse situation than before. What is my problem?

A: Your problem is that you are engaging in what is known as "Emotional Forgetfulness." You forget the emotional pain you experienced when you made poor decisions in the past—when you chose the wrong relationship; when you fell back into a bad habit or addiction. Consequently, you repeated the same pattern or behavior because you only remembered the small initial pleasure you received (which seemed bigger at the time), instead of the large pain that resulted.

The solution is to practice "Right Emotional Memory" before you engage in the self-defeating action: See the pain as it really was. Recall the pain you experienced with the abusive partner; while working in the job that didn't suit your talents; while coming down from the high of an addiction or bad habit.

In life, you have two choices when it comes to creating memories and life patterns. You can choose a little pain now and a lifetime of pleasure. Or, you can choose a little pleasure now and a lifetime of pain.

In the first option, you do the right and disciplined thing. You stick to your weight loss program, you quit the bad habit, you leave the unhealthy relationship. Although you may sacrifice some minor pleasure in the beginning—the extra cake, the smoking, the superficially appealing partner—you end up winning in the long run by feeling healthier, more self-disciplined, and happier.

On the other hand, you can try to obtain a little pleasure now. You may eat too much and exercise too little; you indulge in the bad habit or addiction; you stay in the exciting, but damaging, relationship. When you do this, you have set yourself up for long-term failure and pain because you will keep repeating the same self-defeating actions in a vain attempt to recapture the small pleasure you experienced in the beginning. You will find yourself receiving less pleasure and more pain every time you try to recapture the "mental high" of the past.

With Right Emotional Memory, things will be different. You will remember the pain from your past errors and mistaken choices, and you will not be tempted to go back to the temporary, but false, pleasure of the old ways. Instead, you will choose the more disciplined path that leads you to the lasting pleasure of your own Invincibility.

Q: I understand what you mean about Right Emotional Memory, but I still suffer from my past. I keep thinking about my mistakes. It makes me crazy when I think of how often I have failed, and how many mistakes I have made.

A: Your problem is not your past mistakes—everyone makes mistakes—it's that you condemn yourself for your past mistakes. Regret is what keeps you chained to the past. When you allow yourself to feel regret about a supposed mistake that you made, you create a pressure, a certain type of regret pain. You ask yourself: "What's wrong with me? Why did I do that?"

Then, to relieve the pressure of the regret pain, you tend to act rashly and impulsively—repeating the same mistake, bad habit, or action that got you into trouble in the first place.

The solution is simple: Instead of condemning yourself, and slipping further down the slippery slope of weakness, you need to forgive yourself. When you forgive yourself, you eliminate the "glue" to your past mistakes, and you are free to act differently and freely with a clear mind and spirit. Begin by forgiving yourself for small mistakes or setbacks—you didn't finish the extra task you had planned; you were hot-tempered while in line at the store, you neglected to exercise based on your typical routine.

Learning how to forgive yourself is a step-by-step process. If you're the type of person who finds it hard to forgive yourself, begin by building up your self-forgiveness tolerance. Forgive yourself for small things as you build up your ability to forgive yourself for the more serious regrets in your life related to relationships, career, financial, or lifestyle choices.

How to Truly Relax

Q. Why is it so hard for me to relax?

A: Because you fear the very relaxation you seek. You assume that tension is a power that keeps your life together—for example, you may believe that the Internet and phone are what keep your life moving. You are afraid that if you relax and put away your technological devices for a while, you will lose something valuable—an important communication or opportunity.

In reality, you probably won't miss out on anything terribly important if you take a break from your daily hectic life. In fact, you will probably accomplish more. Relaxation will give you the space you need to see the truth about things; thereby significantly increasing your efficiency and personal power.

When you relax and take a break from fast-paced living, you are more focused and creative—you make fewer mistakes. Once you learn how to give up the negative excitement of tension, you are free to produce more with a relaxed mindset.

Try an experiment: Sit somewhere in a quiet and relaxed setting; perhaps in your home or out in nature. At the same time, take a technology fast. Turn off all of your technological devices and make sure no one disturbs you. Observe your feelings when nothing particularly important is going on in your life—when you are just sitting still and being in the moment. What are you feeling? Are you bored or full of energy? Restless or relaxed?

At this point, the Self-Defeating Mind may try to make you feel nervous. It will try to make you worry that you are missing something important—a crucial call or message. It will warn you that you are not being productive. It will scold you that you are falling further behind in the many things you have to do.

Don't listen to the Self-Defeating Mind's restless voice. Realize that you are doing the right thing by taking care of yourself and your mind.

Continue to sit quietly and let your thoughts come and go without focusing on any of them. When you do this, your feelings of doom and gloom will diminish, and you will find yourself in a lighter and more relaxed state of mind. With practice, you will have a new sense of freedom and joy, and you will attract the truly good things into your life.

Replacing Negativity with Positivity

Q. Why do I put up with the negative in life?

A: You fear that the loss of something negative will leave you with nothing. You are afraid that if you don't have something exciting going on in your life, you will have nothing—you will be bored, lonely, and worthless.

What you may have going on in your life right now is negative excitement—superficial and meaningless activities that may seem fun at first glance, but that ultimately leave you feeling let down, distracted, and even more restless. This negative excitement includes chasing people or external prizes, as well as being addicted to social media, engaging in bad habits and addictions, and participating in idle conversations that lead nowhere.

The irony is that the very negative thing you are afraid of losing, the negative excitement, is what is causing you to feel bored, lonely, and worthless in the first place. You have a tremendous fear of losing the familiar, but false solution.

The good news is that a loss of the false—people and activities who are wrong for you; unhealthy thoughts that attack you—will eventually be replaced by a gain of the true and healthy: compatible relationships, rewarding experiences, and beneficial thoughts.

Start today by making a list of all of the people, situations, thoughts, and circumstances that keep you down and appear to be against you. Perhaps, they are disgruntled friends, sarcastic family members, or self-critical thoughts.

Then make a list of all the people, ideas, and circumstances that are on your side and help you prosper. In this list, you will include like-minded Invincibility-Seeking friends, compassionate and grateful thoughts, and supportive family members or pets.

As you list items in each category, i.e. For or Against, decide that you will substitute one negative element for one positive one every week. As you spend less time with negative people, you will spend more time with affirming and positive people. You will replace negative thoughts and feelings with positive ones: ignorance with insight; heaviness with lightness, and fear with faith.

Soon, you will be on the right track to eliminating negativity in your life and replacing it with consistent and growing positivity, also known as your personal Invincibility.

How to Handle Defeat

Q: My confidence is shattered. I can't reach my goals; I am always frustrated and feel defeated. It seems like my head is destined to hit the wall and there is nothing I can do about it. Why is the whole world against me?

A: I can see why you think that the whole world is against you. In reality, the whole world is not against you. It's You (the Self-Defeating Mind) against You (the Invincible Mind).

The two parts of your mind—negative and positive, healing and harming, winning and defeated—are fighting against each other. It only seems like you're fighting against the world because your thoughts are in conflict with each other. The illusion that you are fighting external obstacles, people, and circumstance is just that: an illusion.

To have more positive results, you need to have more of the Invincible Mind and less of the Self-Defeating Mind. When you live from the Invincible Mind, you rid yourself of old self-defeating habits, and you choose positive habits and lifestyle choices that contribute to your ultimate growth and excellence.

It's impossible to act above your present psychological level. To achieve better results in life, you must improve yourself—the way you see, the way you think, the way you feel. You need to elevate your mindset into one of Invincibility to be equal to the task you have set for yourself—to achieve excellence in your career, finances, relationships, and health.

The best way to raise your mindset is to study and apply these Invincible You principles on a daily basis. It's like learning a new language—the Invincible You language. Each day, you add a new phrase, a new way of thinking, until you are fluent in the most important language of all: Your Invincibility.

How to Find Someone to Love

There is a classic rock song that says, "Can anyone find me somebody to love?"

Many people think like this. They ask the Universe, God, or even other people, to find them somebody to love who will love them back. Many are sorely disappointed. Here's a brief question and answer exchange:

Q: *What if I can't find anyone to love?*

A: Then love yourself and your Don (natural talent).

Q: *What if I'm lonely and need companionship?*

A: Master loneliness within and then you will not crave love and companionship in a yearning state. You will be content within yourself first. While in this state of contentment, you will attract the exact nature of what you are in another human being: happy, loving, and fulfilled.

Incidentally, one of the best ways to master loneliness is by becoming the opposite of lonely—which is loving. Seek out lonely people and offer them your loving energy, support, time, and attention. Help those in need, assist the homeless, and volunteer for charitable and humanitarian groups.

When you do this, you will discover an amazing truth: The more you extend your love without expectation, the more it will return to you. Loneliness will vanish, and love in many forms will take its place in your life.

Happiness and Time

Q: *I'm unhappy. I think I will be happy in the future and that things will change. But, then time passes, and I am as unhappy as ever before. What is the problem?*

A: The problem is that you deceive yourself into thinking that the mere passage of time can make you happy (It won't). In fact, this is a terrible state to live in because you are always thinking that the future will somehow save you. As a result, you rob yourself of the priceless, present moment because you're hoping that you will somehow be happier and more fulfilled in the future.

Let's say that you have suffered pain in the past. You think that time will help ease your pain. Although that may be true in some situations, in most cases time alone doesn't heal wounds.

To regain your happiness, your mind must see things differently. You need to forgive yourself when you have regrets, see the positive in the negative, and resolve to do something different the next time. In other words, act from your Invincible Mind.

By using your mind properly, you can leave a painful experience behind you almost immediately, with few lingering emotional wounds. You can focus on the lesson you learned from the mistake, and you can resolve to act from a higher perspective the next time.

Time is not the deciding factor in recapturing your joy, but your Invincible Mind is. If you want to change your future, change who you are now into a person with an Invincible Mind. When you have the Invincible Mindset, you will be happy—today and tomorrow.

Turn Unfavorable Circumstances into Favorable Ones

Q: *Why do so many unfavorable results come my way?*

A: First of all, you set an unconscious cause into motion—thereby making an unfavorable result an inevitable occurrence. The cause is usually a self-defeating thought, a gloomy idea that "You are not good enough to get what you want." This downward thought then attracts more of its own bad nature such as damaging people and harmful circumstances.

Let's say you're feeling lonely. To escape from your unhappy state, you go out and get involved with the first person who reacts favorably to you. Unfortunately, they may turn out to be an abusive or negative individual. Consequently, your need for emotional relief has prompted you to let your guard down and get involved with a person who is all wrong for you.

Secondly, when something goes wrong, you torment yourself with the question, "Why did this happen?" Instead, you should be asking, "How can I diminish my Self-Defeating Mind so it doesn't happen again?"

The reality is that many people waste a lot of energy in life trying to fulfill the imaginary pictures of their Self-Defeating Mind ("I need to be rich"; "I need to be loved"). The good news is that, once you shed the imaginary pictures of yourself that come from the Self-Defeating Mind, you will be far more efficient, successful, and happy.

Contrary to what you may presently believe, you don't have dozens of problems which cause dozens of unfavorable results. You have one problem, your Self-Defeating Mind, which sets into motion all of the other unfortunate events and circumstances in your life, including bad relationships, poor decision-making, addictions, and bad habits.

Things are different when you live from a unified self, your Invincible Mind. When your mind is centered on growth and inner power, you will rise above unfavorable circumstances, setbacks, and problems. You will become Invincible with a capital "I."

How to Handle Frustration

Q: Why can't I solve my problems no matter what I do? I am always frustrated.

A: When you don't know what to do with a problem, withdraw your attention from it. You will see that anxiety, hopelessness, and suffering don't come from the problem. They come from inside you—from your own Self-Defeating Mind. Your mind is actually the cause of the problem.

Q: But what can I do about that?

A: Realize that you can never fully escape from the problem because you, as the person with the problem, are the problem. Many people mistake an escape for an answer. When they are bored or restless, they anxiously search for some external relief, such as a new love affair, social involvement, financial expenditure, or lifestyle change. This only suspends their nervousness for a short time. They falsely assume that the solution resides outside of themselves.

The real solution *is* to recognize that your Self-Defeating Mind *is* the problem. When you reduce your Self-Defeating Mind—thoughts of weakness, negativity, and defeat—your problems will start to go away as well. To diminish your Self-Defeating Mind, focus on increasing your Invincible Mind by building your Mountain of Invincibility, centering yourself in your Hara, and actualizing your Don (God/nature-given) ability. When you do these things, there will be no longer be a need for you to fight against problems because the "You," Self-Defeating Mind, that was fighting them no longer exists. When the Self-Defeating Mind ceases to exist, your problems will vanish as well.

Q: Can you give me a simple phrase to remember this?

A: Yes, think of it this way: There is no other problem than being what you are, and there is no other solution than in being what you can become.

How to Eradicate Loneliness

Q: How does loneliness work? I feel lonely much of the time.

A: When you feel lonely, you are compelled to do useless and foolish things that you would never do if you were not in this state that you call "loneliness." You get involved with the wrong kind of people and situations to distract yourself. The problem is that when you come home from the party, person, or distracting activity, loneliness is always there, waiting for you.

Q: How do I banish loneliness?

A: Loneliness exists only when you are separated from your true nature, your Invincible Mind. This separation urges you to strive toward self-unity. But the problem is that you strive after the wrong things such as distracting people and superficially exciting experiences. You mistakenly think that these temporary distractions will cure your loneliness. They won't. The only way to cure your loneliness is to unify with your true nature, your Invincible Mind, the essence of you.

To unify yourself, find the practices and activities that nurture you and fill you with love and gratitude, whether it is the arts, time spent in nature with animals or children, physical activity, humanitarian works, creative projects, or a spiritual practice.

Loneliness is cured, not by filling your life with extraneous people and activities, but by healing yourself from the inside out. Find your true Invincible Self, and you will lose loneliness.

What Happiness Truly Is: A Sun That Shines

Q: *Why can't I be consistently happy? Sometimes, I have joyful moments when I acquire something such as a material possession, new friend, or career success, but then I fall back into gloom and despair.*

A: The answer is that you can't be happy with something. You can only be happy, period. When your happiness has an external source, whether it's a person, goal, or circumstance, it is only a temporary flirtation, an illusion that ultimately wears off.

Think of the sun. It is self-sufficient and shines on everyone—the poor, the rich; the beautiful, the not-so-beautiful; the young and the old. If people don't like the sun and cover up, the sun doesn't get upset or disappointed. It simply keeps shining.

In the same way, you can be like the sun and maintain your happy and positive disposition, no matter what is going on around you. You can keep shining your positive energy and light on the world without worrying about whether you will be liked or will receive a benefit. In this way, you rise above the world's problems; you are a star in your own mental galaxy and nothing can hurt you.

Be like the sun, and you will never have to worry about whether you are happy or not. You will just shine everywhere.

How to Deal with One Way Love

Q: *I love someone who doesn't love me back. It's terribly painful. What do I do?*

A: Recognize that this other person represents a need in you such as security, affection, and companionship, which you mistakenly assume is a reality in them. Your fantasy thoughts about the person—not the actual qualities they possess—are what create your craving for the person.

As you raise your level along the Invincible Mind path, you will see the idealized person in a different light. You realize that your needs are internal. Regardless of whether they want you or not, the other person can't supply what you need to make you happy because what you need comes from inside you, not from inside them. When you understand this, your craving for them will fall away, and you will realize that they have nothing to offer your inner self.

Now you will extend your energy outward in a different direction—eventually attracting a person who resonates with your true nature, and with whom, you can build a true Invincible You partnership. In this noble alliance, your mutual goal is to help each other elevate to the highest state of mental and spiritual development as you create a lasting relationship of love and goodness.

Happy Solutions to Life's Problems

Q: *How can I be happy?*

A: Instead of trying to be happy, understand the causes of unhappiness. Stop thinking that you must change conditions before you change yourself. Change yourself and you will naturally change your conditions.

Q: *But, I get so frustrated when I don't see immediate results. What can I do?*

A: Stop despairing over what you can't do in the present moment. Wholeheartedly do whatever you can do right now. Work on fine-tuning your Don, your natural ability. Center yourself in your Hara. Substitute one Invincible Thought (peace) for one Self-Defeating Thought (anger). Always keep in mind that right results come from right efforts—they don't come from wrong efforts or from no efforts at all. Strive to take one step toward your Invincible Mind development each day, and soon you will find that you are on your way to the truth of your excellence.

Q: *But, my life seems so complicated. I have to do so many things to keep it going. How can I change this?*

A: Stop anxiously fighting all of the complications in your life. Simplify your affairs. If you try to do 10 things in one day, you will probably not do any of them very well. Work on doing one thing correctly each day, and you will feel an immediate sense of relief. For example, act despite your fear, spend time meditating on greatness, center yourself in your Hara, and take one small step toward actualizing your Don, your greatest talent. Whatever you do, make sure it's important to you, and that you complete it—doing so will give you a strong sense of satisfaction and confidence.

Q: Why is it that the people I want in my life don't feel the same way about me?

A: Stop trying to win social popularity. Instead, focus on self-acceptance. It is true that you must love yourself before you can truthfully love others, and before they can love you. Accepting yourself is the powerful elixir that releases you from the need to be liked by others.

When you no longer worry about whether you are liked by others, you will paradoxically be liked by many. Your previously intense and desperate desire to be liked and approved of is the very thing that pushed people away from you in the first place. Reverse your focus to self-acceptance, and you will have all of the acceptance from others that you desire.

Q: I search vainly, but I can't find the answers to my life's problems. What can I do?

A: Instead of fighting for answers, be quietly receptive to your Invincible nature. Your Invincible self knows all of the answers—you don't have to do anything except to receive these higher messages.

The frantic chasing and searching for the right way to live is the very thing that keeps you from finding the correct path. It's like the fish who is frantically searching for water and doesn't realize it is already in the water; the water is all around it. Once it relaxes and sees the true situation, everything becomes clear.

At this point, you will recognize the truth: You don't need to search for answers anymore because you *are* the answers—all of which originate from your Invincible Mind.

You can stop searching. You have arrived at your final destination: Love, success, and happiness.

Chapter Twenty-One

....

Begin Your Invincible Life

You are on your way to becoming Invincible. As you travel higher up the Invincible You Mountain, you will see that your life is transforming as you help transform the lives of those around you. As you learn these principles, you may be asking yourself: How do I know that I am making progress?

Here are some clues:

- *You have more consistency of effort.* You keep on track in your Invincibility work for longer periods of time. You have more patience, discipline, and desire to reach your self-development goals such as being happier, more loving, and more authentic. You become a true mental magician as you control not only what you want, but also what you don't want—the Self-Defeating Mind.

- *You are calm when you realize that your Self-Defeating nature tries to shove itself back into your life.* You see its mechanical movements as it tries to bring you down. The good news is that your new Invincible Mindset maintains full awareness of the Self-Defeating Mind's deceptions. You can stop it at its own game by saying, "No," when it tries to enter you.

- *You don't stop working on yourself when things are going well.* You know that you will have down moments; times of temptation, weakness, and doubt. The Self-Defeating Mind has been with you for 20, 30, 40, 50, 60, or more years, and won't let go of you that easily. The good news is that you now have powerful weapons at your disposal to defeat the Self-Defeating Mind. You have awareness of the way the Self-Defeating Mind works, and best of all, you have the supreme taste of the Invincible Mind. Once you have sampled the power and beauty of the Invincible Mind, you will not be so attracted to the fake or artificial. You will want the Invincible Mind with you on a daily basis.

■ *You rise above petty dissatisfactions.* When your life is dominated by the Self-Defeating Mind, many things can bother you: a friend's snide remark, a traffic jam, a computer malfunction, a loved one's critical comment. When you live from the Self-Defeating Mind, many things make you feel mad, sad, or scared. You can't help yourself because the Self-Defeating Mind creates a haunted house in your mind that dominates your thoughts.

On the other hand, things are much different when you see things from your Invincible Mind. Now the things that used to bother you—critical comments from negative people, mechanical malfunctions, temporary delays and obstacles—seem trivial and unimportant to you. With your new Invincible Mindset, you realize that you are neither your choices, nor your desires. Your true essence is something much higher: It is based on recognizing your Invincible Self: the You that is powerful, confident, loving, and happy despite the obstacles and challenges you face.

As you become more of the Invincible You, you will be able to help others make their own journey to excellence and happiness. The beautiful part of the Invincible You Life is that it is one of harmony, sharing, and connection with your fellow human beings.

You will not be lonely when you build your life on Invincible You principles because your aim is to spread love to others without expectation. You are helpful and loving to others, not because you want to win their approval, liking, or love, but because you are a naturally giving and loving person who is extending your positive energy outwardly.

Now, as you climb up the Invincible You Mountain, and begin to live a life that is truly worth living, you will come to an amazing realization: Invincibility was always within you. You simply needed to recognize who you were: A person of strength, beauty, love, and power.

Congratulations. You are about to graduate from Invincible U— Invincible University. It's your turn now to take your education and help transform the world as you transform yourself. Blessings and love on your journey to the real you.

Invincible Me

One day I saw the person I wanted to be;
but they were smarter, stronger, and better than me.
I felt envious; why couldn't I be?
They stood strong; I stood weak.
They were victorious; I felt defeat.
But, then as I looked closer, I saw things from a different perspective:
I realized I was only looking at a clouded reflection.
In reality, there was never anyone else. It was always me.
At last I saw the truth: I am Invincible. I am Free.

GLOSSARY

Action Despite the Thought: The concept of going for what you want despite the fear thoughts that are attacking you: "I will look foolish; I will lose if I go after what I want." Action despite the thought liberates you from self-doubt and procrastination and gives you the momentum you need to achieve lasting success.

Action Is Distilled Intent: Your action, or behavior, is what matters in the end. It's not what you say you will do, or what you think about doing, it's what you actually end up doing that counts the most.

Anger Dissociation: An exercise in which you observe your anger without identifying with it—without thinking that it is you.

Anger Weakness: This is the fiery thought that makes you explode with anger when you think that others are disrespecting you, or that life is unfair. It is the erroneous belief that you are not getting the respect, attention, or credit you deserve—resulting in touchiness, frustration, anger, and even violence.

Art of Reversal: A new approach to getting better results in life: doing the opposite of what you have been doing, or what is generally expected. Reversal gives you a different "out of the box" perspective that liberates your mind to come up with new solutions.

Be Like The Sun: Wherever you go, be like the sun and radiate your goodness and loving warmth to all—without expecting anything in return. By doing so, you will attract the right people and circumstances into your life.

Blast Off Mentality: When you exert all of your psychological energy to burst through initial obstacles until you achieve a free-flowing momentum to achieve your goals.

Centerpoint: The balance or midpoint between different states of life and mind. Between arrogance and self-doubt, there is confidence. Between aggression and submission, there is self-respect. Between sadness and happiness, there is maturity. Living from the Centerpoint gives you depth of character and perspective.

Desert of Weakness: The holding place for all of the negative, critical, and self-attacking thoughts that have built up inside your mind over the years—including Rush, Anger, Regret, Futility, and Fear. In this underground nightmare, you are trapped by bad habits and compulsions, perceived inadequacies, and self-demeaning thoughts and feelings.

Contraction Mindset: This is the mindset in which your life energy gets weaker and smaller; when you are swept away by negative emotions such as anger, sadness, or regret.

Don: This is your God-given (nature-given) ability; your secret wellspring of ability, power, and skill that is unique to your psychological DNA. You were born with this talent and can use it to improve your life and the lives of others.

Energy Pool: The store of emotional energy you have for different tasks and life activities. Daily, you draw on different pools for your energy needs: work, relationships, entertainment, and relaxation.

Enjoy the Easy Roll of Life: With this perspective, instead of chasing people or circumstances, you let the things you want come to you naturally.

Expansion Mindset: With this way of thinking, you are always looking to grow and contribute. You see life as an ever-increasing miracle of opportunities to experience, love, and learn.

Family of Weakness: These are the negative thoughts in your mind, such as Fear and Anger, as represented by a mental family of gossiping and critical relatives who get together for a family disunion.

Fear to Reality Journal: In this exercise, you write down all of the things you are afraid of, and then check periodically to see if they have come true. Once you realize that most of what you feared didn't occur in the way you expected, you will begin to liberate yourself from many of the fears that torment you on a daily basis.

Fear Weakness: This is the foundation of many other weaknesses. Loneliness is the fear of being alone; depression is the fear of losing something valuable; anger contains the fear of being frustrated or treated poorly. The Fear Weakness is an exaggerated, and often unrealistic, fear about bad things that may never happen—tormenting you about things that have a small chance of occurring in reality.

Futility Weakness: This is the thought that you are being deprived of the good things in life; that you are living beneath your potential, and you are doomed to be a failure.

Generosity Week: For a one-week period, focus on giving fully of yourself to others—not just money—but time, energy, advice, love, attention, and that rare, special gift: Listening. This will not only benefit others, but also yourself, as you feel grateful for all of the help you can give to those you care about.

Get Your Fools Out: An exercise in which you intentionally act foolish and silly in an exaggerated way in private, so you can be more relaxed and confident in public.

Gift of Negativity: This is a false "gift" that isn't really a gift: criticism, resentment, anger, gossip, and fear. You can refuse the so-called gift, and it returns to the giver.

Go for it Principle: This is when you go for what you truly want in life, even though you're not sure you will get it. Even if you don't accomplish your goal initially, simply trying for what you want is the very action that opens the doors to tremendous success in your life.

Hands of Harmony: An Anger Weakness reduction exercise in which you create a harmonious flow of physical motion with your partner that is matched by your verbal harmonizing with them.

Hands of Love: An exercise in which you imagine that your hand contains hundreds of individual loving minds, each having an intelligence of its own. When you shake people's hands, you visualize that you are passing loving energy to them through your hands.

Hara: The physical point that lies two inches below your navel and represents your life energy—your power, stability, balance, and intuition.

How Thinker: A resilient individual who is always thinking about how to stage a comeback after a momentary setback. If they see that their happiness is being limited, they find the block—the bad habit or negative people—and they remove it.

If Thinker: A person who feels defeated and has a sense of futility about achieving their dreams. Feeling sorry for themselves, they say, "If only I had done this better." As a result, the next time they try something, they already feel defeated.

Invincibility Blueprint: A detailed plan to your inner and outer excellence that consists of instilling positive habits, thoughts, and emotions to rewire your brain and bring you maximum results.

Invincible Mind: The part of your mind that thinks and acts like a champion—with continually expanding thoughts of confidence, love, gratitude, joy, and excellence. It gives you a sense of continual elevation in which you surpass obstacles and rise above negative emotional states to achieve lasting success.

Invincible Mind Family: The positive and healthy side of your mental family. There is "Papa Joy" on one side of the table, and sitting next to him is "Mama Compassion." These light and healing forces in your life are powerful, good, and benevolent. These are the positive and healing thought guides that you can draw from to reach true happiness.

Invincible Mountain: The beautiful mental peak where you find peace, joy, love, confidence, and contentment. Not a physical territory or land, it is a special place in your mind that is free from self-defeating thoughts, and full of all the inner power you need to live to your greatest potential.

Invincibility Seekers: Invincibility Seekers are those individuals who strive to be the best they can possibly be. They focus on mastering their inner states of being and creating thoughts of compassion, empathy, love, creativity, and confidence—to elevate themselves and others.

LoveQ: A new form of higher intelligence based on loving energy and maximizing human potential. LoveQ contains essential psychological and spiritual characteristics—compassion, empathy, kindness, patience, generosity, and gentleness—that make up a whole and healthy human being.

Loving Energy Without Expectation: Give love to others—be nice and kind—without expecting anything in return. Instead of trying to get something from other people, you are content within yourself. As a result, you attract the people and circumstances that resonate with who you really are.

Loving Money Energy (LME): A new way to think of money—as a loving energy force that travels between human beings to enhance the lives of those it touches, and to make the world a better place.

Mastermind Group. A union of like-minded people with a certain expertise who meet regularly to exchange ideas, support each other, and solve mutual problems.

Mental Bath: A visualization exercise accompanied by a bath or shower that helps you get rid of accumulated negative energy from others and the environment.

Mental Pathmaker: A person who creates new positive habits through repetition. Each time they repeat the same desirable habit, they make the mental path (mental connection to the habit) deeper and wider.

Mind of Abundance: The Mind of Abundance is the belief that you will have all the money you need, and that the world will work in your favor to bring you the financial security you desire.

Mind of Patience: The mindset that that there is always enough time to do what needs to be done. The opposite of the Rush Weakness.

Mind of Scarcity: This is the fear that you won't have enough money in life, or that you will lose what little you have. With this mindset, you may not take smart business risks because you are more afraid of what you have to lose than what you have to gain.

Monkey Mind: The chattering voices in your head that warn you about all the problems you will be facing.

Negativity Seekers: Individuals who reside at a low psychological level of development—critical, complaining, negative, selfish, and aggressive. Although they may appear pleasant at first, these emotionally draining people can make your existence a living hell.

Neurotic Village: A mental place full of misery, pain, competition, anger, fear, and regret. With this mindset, you don't feel like you're succeeding, regardless of what you accomplish in the world.

One-Point Hara Focus: When you maintain complete and utter concentration on your primary focus or mission in life. It means being guided by your Hara (gut or instinct) and maintaining a laser-like focus on what you want to accomplish.

Pain Gap: The gap between the way you are now—trapped by negative thoughts—and the way you want to be: A happy and healthy person. Once you go through the pain gap, you will be on the side of your own Invincibility.

Power of Discard: An exercise for discarding mental and physical junk. By throwing away negative ideas and obsolete items, a fresh mind can be acquired and positive energy can be generated.

Power of Spontaneity: An innovative response to a new situation, a force for inner development, and the energy behind joy, creativity, and laughter.

Play All the Keys on the Mental Piano: Instead of getting caught up in a one-note response to life—anger, regret, or fear—you fully experience many different kinds of feelings such as happiness, joy, gratitude, and compassion. In the process, you develop balance, harmony, and flexibility.

Regret Weakness: This is the thought that you blew it in life and made an unforgivable mistake. The Regret Weakness torments you for past follies and errors, and makes you believe that you are a failure who will keep repeating the same mistakes.

Re-Imprinting Experience: An exercise in which you mentally relive a previous painful experience from a more mature perspective. Instead of feeling regret about the past situation, you imprint the lesson you learned in your mind. The result is that you become a more loving person—toward yourself and others.

Relentless Confidence: This is the heightened state of self-belief that leads you to excellence. It is a thought-shift toward the things—people, circumstances, and higher power—that are *for* you, instead of the things that are *against* you.

Mountain of Invincibility: The part of your mind that holds positive thoughts including creativity, compassion, gratitude, gentleness, patience, and love. This is where you draw sustenance for daily challenges; where you generate enthusiasm, momentum, and persistence.

Reverse Birthday: In this exercise, you will reverse the typical birthday tradition and give gifts to your loved ones and friends. Doing so will bring you the gift of gratefulness for the people in your life.

Reverse Giving: Giving away what you most want to receive. It is a powerful technique for dissolving your feelings of deprivation, envy, and frustration, and filling yourself with feelings of contentment, gratitude, and joy.

Reverse Lesson: When you learn to do the opposite of what a Negativity Seeker does: You learn the importance of peace from an angry person, patience from an impatient person, and love from an unloving person.

Rush Weakness: The thought that you don't have enough time to do what you need to do. The Rush Weakness pressures you to hurry and frantically run around to get the answers and results you need—frustration and irritation often follow.

Self-Defeating Mind: The part of your mind that is easily defeated because it dwells on the negative, the bad, and the failures of life. When your Self-Defeating Mind is in charge, you miss opportunities, or if you see them, you don't have the willpower or courage to take action. It wants you to fail.

Seven Percent Club of the Living: You are part of the select few who are currently alive on Earth at the present time. Rejoice: You are alive and have the opportunity to do everything you have always wanted to do in your life.

Spiritual Vacation: A state of mental relaxation in which you go through your day as if you were on an actual physical vacation. In this relaxed state of mind, you enjoy every moment of every day as you participate in life with joy and power.

Sexual Transmutation: The utilization of sexual energy for creative, humanitarian, and spiritual purposes—it's the investment of sexual energy in a person, activity, or idea for a higher purpose.

Three Tries: The three-part roadmap to success: 1. Meditate on Greatness (learn from those who have already made it where you want to go). 2. Reverse Your Trying (do the opposite of what you've been doing to receive the opposite of what you've been getting). 3. Try for your Don (aim to enhance and share your God/nature given talent).

Walk in the Light: To live a kindhearted and truthful life in which you focus on spreading goodness in the world.

REFERENCES

Bhagwan, D. (2016). *Brahmacharya: Celibacy with understanding* (Abr.) (In English). Adalaj, Gandhinagar, India: Dada Bhagwan Aradhana Trust.

Desjardins, J. (2017). All of the world's money and markets in one visualization. Retrieved from http://www.visualcapitalist.com/worlds-money-markets-one-visualization-2017/

Dewall, C., Lambert, N., Pond, R., Kashdan, T., & Fincham, F. (2011). A grateful heart is a nonviolent heart. *Social Psychological and Personality Science, 3(2),* 232-240. doi:10.1177/1948550611416675

Digdon, N., & Koble, A. (2011). Effects of constructive worry, imagery distraction, and gratitude interventions on sleep quality: A pilot trial. *Applied Psychology: Health and Well-Being, 3(2),* 193-206. doi:10.1111/j.1758-0854.2011.01049.x

Ford, B., Shallcross, A., Mauss, I., Floerke, V., & Gruber, J. (2014). Desperately seeking happiness: Valuing happiness is associated with symptoms and diagnosis of depression. *Journal of Social and Clinical Psychology, 33(10),* 890-905. doi:10.1521/jscp.2014.33.10.890

Haub, C. (1995). How many people have ever lived on earth? *Population Today, Feb. 23 (2),* 4-5. PubMed PMID: 12288594

Kashdan, T., Barrett, L., & McKnight, P. (2015). Unpacking emotion differentiation. *Current Directions in Psychological Science, 24(1),* 10-16. doi:10.1177/096372141455070

Seligman, M., & Beagley, G. (1975). Learned helplessness in the rat. *Journal of Comparative and Physiological Psychology, 88(2)*, 534-541. doi:10.1037/h0076430

Shaffer, J. (2012). Neuroplasticity and positive psychology in clinical practice: A review for combined benefits. *Psychology, 03(12)*, 1110-1115. doi:10.4236/psych.2012.312a164

The Myers & Briggs Foundation. (2018). How frequent is my type? Retrieved from https://www.myersbriggs.org/my-mbti-person-ality-type/my-mbti-results/how-frequent-is-my-type.htm

About

DR. ALEXANDER AVILA

Dr. Alexander Avila holds four graduate degrees, including a Ph.D. in clinical psychology. He is the bestselling author of LoveTypes (Avon Books/HarperCollins) and *The Gift of Shyness* (Simon and Schuster). *LoveTypes* is the first book to teach readers how to find their compatible soul mate from among the 16 Myers-Briggs personality types. Over 40 million Internet users have applied Dr. Avila's *LoveType* system to find lasting love. *The Gift of Shyness* has broken new ground by showing shy and Introverted singles how to embrace their Introversion and Shyness to develop social confidence and attract their ideal love partner.

As a respected college professor, researcher, and presenter, Dr. Avila has shared his findings with students, academics, and professionals in the fields of psychology and human behavioral sciences.

An acclaimed TV and Radio Personality, Dr. Avila is the creator of the award-winning show, *Love University*, in which listeners learn how to love themselves, others, and a higher power. He has appeared on numerous media outlets such as *CNN, ABC, CBS, and Telemundo*, and has been featured in *Cosmopolitan, Glamour, Latina, Today's*

Black Woman, Real Health, Woman's World, and the *Los Angeles Times*, among other publications.

On a personal note, Dr. Avila enjoys salsa dancing, chess, books, good-hearted people, martial arts, animals, nature, and spirituality.

Dr. Avila's mission is to help humanity transform pain into power and to extend loving energy to the world. Dr. Avila can be reached at www.loveuniversity.love and loveuniversitylove@gmail.com.

LISTEN TO AMERICA'S TOP LOVE TRANSFORMATION PODCAST

Dr. Avila's

LOVE UNIVERSITY

EVERY WEDNESDAY AT NOON

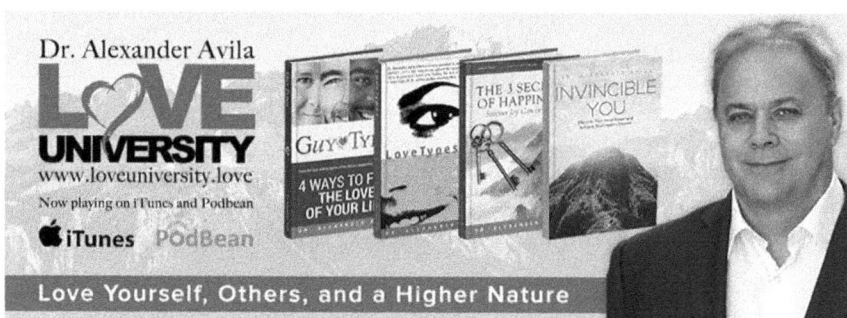

NOW ON MULTIPLE PLATFORMS:

LISTEN ON ITUNES: https://apple.co/2KMhRbe
LISTEN ON PODBEAN: loveuniversity.podbean.com
LISTEN ON SOUNDCLOUD: http://bit.ly/2MtkuSD
LISTEN ON SPOTIFY: https://spoti.fi/2Z1bbyV

www.loveuniversity.love

Join Dr. Avila each week for a fun and practical weekly lesson on self-empowerment and love on his hit podcast, *Love University*.

In school you learned about grammar, history, science, and math, but, chances are, you weren't educated on some of the most important things in life: love, relationships, success, and happiness.

In *Love University*, Dr. Avila teaches you how to achieve mastery in your relationships, finances, career, health, and emotional well-being. Utilizing a unique blend of positive psychology, practical spirituality, and plain old common sense, *Love University* shows you how to love yourself, others, and a higher nature.

Some of the popular topics include:

- *The Psychology of Wealth: How to Have the Mind of Abundance*

- *Find Your Mate With the Power of Personality Type*

- *Co-Dependency for Dummies: Set Yourself Free*

- *Humor IQ: Laugh Your Way to Joy and Success*

- *The Power of Self-Discipline: The Might to Do Right*

- *The Abuse-Free Life: Declare Your Emotional Freedom*

- *Personal Spirituality: Your Path to Joy and Inner Power*

- *Be the Ruler of Technology, Not Its Servant*

Listen each Wednesday as Dr. Avila, the Professor of the Heart, and his celebrity guests, entertain, educate, and enlighten you on the secrets of love, success, and happiness.

Love University is now in session.

GET THE BOOK THAT WILL CHANGE YOUR LIFE: *THE 3 SECRETS OF HAPPINESS: FOREVER JOY CAN BE YOURS*

In the mold of *The Alchemist* and *The Teachings of Don Juan, The 3 Secrets of Happiness: Forever Joy Can be Yours* by bestselling author and psychologist, Dr. Alexander Avila, inspires you to leave behind what has trapped you and achieve your highest self.

The 3 Secrets of Happiness is a modern fable about a pompous psychiatrist, Harry, who goes to interview (for his next bestselling book) a mountain hermit, Tanaka—a mysterious personage who is alleged to know the secrets of happiness. Stubborn and filled with his own hidden pain, the psychiatrist receives more than he bargained for as he comes under the tutelage of the spunky, yet wise, Tanaka. In the end, the psychiatrist abandons his false self and finds peace and love by transforming his destiny through *The 3 Secrets of Happiness*: Gratitude, Joyful Optimism, and Forgiveness.

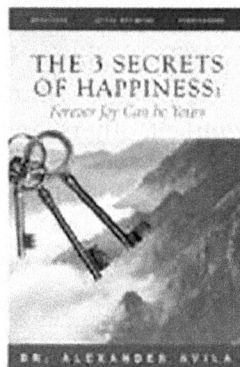

Now it's your turn. Are you ready to learn the *3 Secrets of Happiness* and live your heart's desires?

You will never be the same again.

TO DISCOVER YOUR TRUE HAPPINESS, GO HERE TO PURCHASE YOUR COPY OF *THE 3 SECRETS OF HAPPINESS*:

www.loveuniversity.love/books

JOIN THE "TYPE COMMUNITY" AND FIND THE LOVE OF YOUR LIFE

Now there's a way to win the love game and find the right man for you: It's called *GuyTypes*.

In *GuyTypes*, bestselling author and award-winning psychologist, Dr. Alexander Avila, introduces a revolutionary new love finding paradigm. Streamlining his classic bestseller *LoveTypes* (over 40 million followers), and combining social networking with Myers-Briggs Type compatibility, Dr. Avila unveils a groundbreaking system for finding true love in our fast-paced technological world. In *GuyTypes*, you will discover what you truly want in a mate and how to get it. Here are the four *GuyTypes* (romantic styles) who can light your fire and keep it burning. One of these will be your perfect match (you will learn which one):

Meaning Seeker (NF): 13.5% of the male population. If you've ever wanted to be romanced like a goddess, then this is the right guy for you. Sensitive, imaginative, artistic, philosophical, poetic, and a true romantic: He is the lover of all lovers.

Knowledge Seeker (NT): 14.8% of the male population. You've met your "Iron Man": Brilliant, powerful, innovative, and ultimately successful. His incredible brainpower will stimulate your mind (and body), and his incisive and witty take on life will keep you intrigued and fascinated.

Security Seeker (SJ): 43.1% of the male population. You've found your rock: steady, reliable, traditional, and family-orientated. He is the loyal husband and loving father who will be by your side for life; there is nothing he won't do for you and the family he loves.

Excitement Seeker (SP): 28.6% of the male population. Get ready and fasten your seatbelts—the fun is about to begin. This charismatic and confident guy will bring as much fun, laughter, and enjoyment into your life together as humanly possible.

Once you know the right guy for you, you will learn how to:

*Quickly profile his personality type by asking 3 Magic questions or making micro-observations about his behavior.

*Use Personality Networking and the latest social media tools to break the ice and get to know him.

*Win his heart by tapping into his unique personality type preferences.

*Rate his sexual compatibility (including cheating risk), fatherhood ability, and long-term relationship potential.

*Develop a lasting relationship and marriage with the love of your life.

TO FIND THE MAN OF YOUR DREAMS, GO HERE TO
PURCHASE YOUR COPY OF *GUYTYPES*:

www.loveuniversity.love/books

READ THE BOOK
THAT STARTED THE DATING
REVOLUTION AND FIND YOUR
SOUL MATE TODAY:
LOVETYPES: DISCOVER YOUR
ROMANTIC STYLE AND FIND
YOUR SOUL MATE

Now there's a solution to incompatible dates and failed relationships: It's called *LoveTypes: Discover Your Romantic Style and Find Your Soul Mate* by Dr. Alexander Avila.

With over 40 million followers, and more than 20 years of proven love compatibility results, *LoveTypes* is your go-to guide to help you find your soul mate from among the crowd of potential suitors. Dr. Avila has revolutionized the dating world by applying the theory behind the Myers-Briggs Type Indicator®—the most popular personality test in the world—to teach readers how to find their most compatible partner from among the 16 LoveTypes, or romantic styles.

By taking a brief quiz, you first determine your unique LoveType profile. From there, the system guides you toward the best LoveType for you and provides specific answers to your most pressing relationship questions:

*Which of the 16 *LoveTypes* is most compatible with me—psychologically, emotionally, and sexually?

*What four questions can I ask to determine instantly if someone is right for me?

*Where can I meet my ideal mate?

*What dating strategies will win the heart of my ideal LoveType and ensure a long-term relationship?

Lasting love no longer has to be hit or miss with *LoveTypes*, your complete and indispensable guide to a happy and fulfilling romantic life.

TO FIND YOUR COMPATIBLE SOUL MATE TODAY, GO HERE
TO PURCHASE YOUR COPY OF ***LOVETYPES***:
www.loveuniversity.love/books

RECEIVE YOUR FREE ONE YEAR SUBSCRIPTION TO THE "INVINCIBLE YOU EZINE"

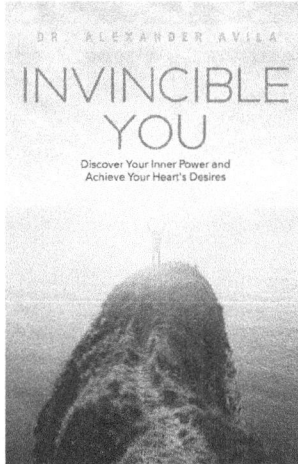

GO TO (https://www.loveuniversity.love/free-gift/) and receive your FREE monthly transformational "INVINCIBLE YOU EZINE."

Each month, you will receive the latest research-proven tips, strategies, and findings for achieving personal invincibility and attaining success in your career, finances, health, relationships, and happiness. Dr. Avila will be your personal mentor and guide as you learn how to reach your highest potential and love yourself, others, and the highest possibilities of life.

www.ingramcontent.com/pod-product-compliance
Lightning Source LLC
Chambersburg PA
CBHW071116090426
42737CB00030B/1475